HATCH
Leap
SOAR

HATCH *Leap* SOAR

Your Three Steps to Total
Fulfillment, Real Success
and True Happiness

By LaToyia Dennis

Mango Publishing
CORAL GABLES

Cover Design: Roberto Núñez
Cover Photo: Zamurovic Photography (Shutterstock)
Layout & Design: Liz Hong

For permission requests, please contact the publisher at:
Mango Publishing Group
2850 S Douglas Road, 2nd Floor
Coral Gables, FL 33134 USA
info@mango.bz

For special orders, quantity sales, course adoptions and corporate sales, please email the publisher at sales@mango.bz. For trade and wholesale sales, please contact Ingram Publisher Services at customer.service@ingramcontent.com or +1.800.509.4887.

Hatch Leap Soar: Your 3-Steps to Total Fulfillment, Real Success and True Happiness

Library of Congress Cataloging-in-Publication number: 2019935678
ISBN: (print) 978-1-63353-952-5, (ebook) 978-1-63353-953-2
BISAC category code SEL027000, SELF-HELP / Personal Growth / Success

Printed in the United States of America

This book is dedicated to the memory of my grandmother, Shirley L. Dean. She always knew that I would eventually hatch, leap, and soar, well before I ever believed I could.

"It may be hard for an egg to turn into a bird: it would be a jolly sight harder for it to learn to fly while remaining an egg. We are like eggs at present. And you cannot go on indefinitely being just an ordinary, decent egg. We must be hatched or go bad."

—C. S. Lewis

Table of Contents

Foreword

"It is one of the beautiful compensations of life that no man can sincerely try to help another without helping himself."

—Ralph Waldo Emerson

Meeting LaToyia for the first time, it is impossible not to be inspired by her indomitable spirit. She has made a total commitment to be about service. When you hear her story, you find it hard to believe this beautiful, articulate, and educated wife and mother lived and persevered, even flourished, through these circumstances.

First, she understood that we cannot change our yesterdays, but we can definitely change our tomorrows. Second, our circumstances are not a life sentence.

Her desire to empower and uplift women, especially mothers, to understand the magnitude of their responsibilities to their children and all children has led her to take a pen in hand. LaToyia now writes. She writes to encourage, she writes to empower and to uplift. She calls us all to turn on the light inside of us. May we follow her lead and Hatch, Leap, and Soar to amazing heights.

—Rose Rock

Preface

At the beginning of each year, I select one word to focus on. *Hatch*, *leap*, and *soar* were my words from 2014 to 2016. When I chose the word *hatch* in 2014, I had no idea how it would start a complete life overhaul and personal transformation for me.

The focus on transformation is at the heart of this book, *Hatch, Leap, Soar*. It is the concept of becoming who you were created to be. The idea of reaching total fulfillment, real success, and true happiness is subjective. You have to determine what those ideals mean to you. What is sure to happen, in order for you to find your own personal nirvana, are hatching, leaping, and soaring. However, all three stages of change do not happen just once. Over the course of your life, you will be hatching in some areas, leaping and taking a chance in others, while soaring in others. The process is beautiful. I relate the process to that of a baby bird inside an egg, ready to…

Hatch.

Before you can begin to change and start realizing your potential, you may find yourself safely settled in your comfort zone. In essence, you are stuck inside your shell. When you begin the process of hatching, you are defying the norm, pressing past your fears to break free. Once you've hatched, you will be able to see the possibilities ahead. Your mind will be open to achieving something you were born to do. You start to think, *As soon as I get out of here, I will be able to do anything I set my mind to.* But to literally break out of your shell, you will have to make a…

Leap.

You may take a leap of faith or a leap in a completely different direction than you have ever gone before. It is important to have faith that you are better off freed from your shell than you are stuck inside. Take the chance to propel out of your current comfort zone.

To reach the potential that everyone is given, step toward it. Opportunities and change will not suddenly materialize while you are sitting alone in your shell. Move, shake or dance—do anything that will allow you to experience life as never before. A bird cannot learn to fly by sitting pretty in its nest. A bird has to leap to learn how to…

Soar.

When you discover how to break free of the barriers you have built up over the years, you will soon soar toward the realm of your personal possibilities. You can fulfill your dreams by taking steps, one at a time, until you are soaring into higher regions. Once you take wing, your life will be transformed.

Section One

Hatch

Chapter One

Understanding

*"Your pain is the breaking of the shell that
encloses your understanding."*

—Khalil Gibran

W hat first comes to mind when you read the word *hatch*? Most people imagine a baby bird hatching from its shell. On the surface, you would be spot-on. But I believe hatching is so much more. It is a process of *becoming.* I love this definition of *hatch*: "an opening of a restricted size allowing for passage from one area to another."

I would venture to bet that you, along with thousands of other people, have a shared desire to live in a way that is meaningful. We all want to better understand our overall purpose in this thing called life. But that nugget of comprehension can be the most difficult thing for you to figure out. Then, taking the next steps to achieve it is a whole other dilemma. Not understanding how to reach your purpose can grow to be a constant underlying source of irritation, frustration, and even personal pain.

I have learned that, in due time and under the right set of circumstances, the very pain of this discomfort can, and oftentimes will, lead ultimately to an internal quest for understanding. By definition, *understanding* means "to have a mental grasp of or knowledge about a situation or how something works." And isn't that just what you are trying to figure out? The ultimate question you may be asking yourself is, *How was I designed to contribute to the world? How do I take*

what I am and what I have and contribute my gifts to the world,
all while finding a sense of fulfillment for myself?

I am not sure about you, but once I really am able to wrap my mind around an idea, there is no stopping me. Have you ever been uncertain about how to proceed and then received clarity on a matter? How much more are you able and willing to do once you gain understanding?

Since life is meant to be progressive, you are continually charged with reaching new levels, which means that you should continually seek new understandings. In fact, you are uniquely created to evolve and develop in different seasons than the person sitting next to you. It is only the failure to understand how that evolution works that can lead to an experience a sense of discomfort and pain in your life.

That pain is not meant to take you out; instead it is meant to *break you out!* That pain forces you to become uncomfortable to the point of doing whatever is necessary to get out of the place and space where you feel stuck. I believe that life is strategically designed so that you will ultimately arrive in a place where the pain and discomfort get to be so difficult that they push you to find understanding and clarity on how to move forward.

Within your consciousness lives a record of all of your past victories, defeats, and milestones that you have encountered throughout your life's journey. There will be distinct moments when you will feel a prompting to press beyond into something new. This draw will lead you down the path to understanding. You can grasp the knowledge of who you are and who you have the potential to become.

If you let it, this feeling will pull you along until you realize how the things that you have learned and experienced are a part of the next level of your growth. This deep desire to find a place of understanding is the crack in your shell. It is the preparation you need for hatching and stepping out on your journey toward true fulfillment.

Hatching is about breaking through the internal shell of your life and leaving the familiar space where you usually exist. Only when you push yourself out of your comfort zone do you find an opportunity for greatness. Hatching is about recognizing that none of us were ever intended to remain in one place, or at the same level, in our lives. We all have gifts, talents, passions, and abilities that are meant to grow and develop in their own season.

When I began to think about the word *hatch*, I was in what I thought was a settled season of my life. I was comfortable, carrying out my day-to-day tasks and accomplishing what came naturally to me. I did not realize at the time that my predictable everyday lifestyle was the very shell from which I needed to hatch. Looking back, there were signs that my soul was seeking something new. You may be wondering, *What is the problem with having a predictable life? I have a routine, I follow it, and I meet the marks that have been set for me.* Here is the difference—if you do these things in a mundane fashion, with a lack of passion, like the path I had started to take, then plain and simple, you need to hatch. Looking back now, there were plenty of signs that my soul was seeking something new.

For me, the signs began with the unusually strong feeling of hope that came over me as I was compiling my list of New Year's resolutions. Even though I had no idea what the coming year would bring, I felt a spark of excitement. Somehow, this year would be different. I felt that this was going to be the year for me. There was no way for me to know the journey of self-discovery that would unfold as I followed my heart's direction. I had no idea that it was my time to hatch. There was no way to know that what would be different this year was me!

If you asked any of my friends and work colleagues, they would say that I was meant to be a fundraiser because I have worked for some amazing organizations and raised millions of dollars. However, I have since found that fundraising is not the only thing that I was purposed to do. To be honest, I am not sure if fundraising was *ever* the path I was meant to follow, even though I was more than capable to do the job.

As I continue to grow and learn while experiencing the phenomenon called life, I share this lesson as a result of my continual process and understanding of hatching. I am not sure that we as individuals are purposed to do something *just* because we are good at it. More so, I am inclined to believe that there are many things that we are called to do if we want to live our most fulfilled lives.

For example, my fundraising has impacted the futures of children and countless of people around the world, and I am very proud of all that I have done. However, I know also that I was purposed to be a mother, wife, and mentor and to play many other roles. Even though I have encountered these responsibilities at different seasons of my life, they have all been a part of my pathway to purpose.

This process can be compared to a bird that begins its life as a newborn baby, but ultimately grows through various stages. We are all called to transform and grow from one stage to the next. And, most likely, you will receive a signal, either internally or externally, when it is time to move out of your comfort zone or protective space. Motivational speaker Leslie Calvin "Les" Brown once said, "If you put yourself in a position where you have to stretch outside of your comfort zone, then you are forced to expand your consciousness." I wholeheartedly agree.

> *"If you put yourself in a position where you have to stretch outside your comfort zone, then you are forced to expand your consciousness."*
>
> —Les Brown

The process of hatching is about accepting the call of your next purpose. It is about:

- Recognizing when the time is right to move out of your comfort zone.

- Self-discovery and learning the move is just one level up at a time.

- Intuition and responsiveness to the spirit inside of you to be all that you were created to be.

I love the army's affirmation, "Be All That You Can Be." To me, that's exactly what it means to hatch! You are allowing a space that has become restricted to open up for the possibility of more. You are tapping into the special place in your mind that ignites the desire to break the shells of limitations, fears, doubts, and restrictions to become the best version of yourself.

One of the key indicators that you may be entering a season of hatching is that you begin to experience a sense of dissatisfaction with your current status. This can happen all of a sudden, or perhaps you feel it beginning to brew over time, but somehow you start to feel as if something is missing or needs to change.

I clearly recall when I first entered the place of hatching and how I was confronted with feelings of duality. Even though I had a full load of A-list clients and was indeed an expert in my field, there was still a nagging truth that I had to face. All of a sudden, I felt as if there was something missing in my day-to-day routine. I started having an ongoing internal conversation with myself that always ended with, *I know that there is more I should be doing.* And, even if I did not say it out loud, I was growing weary of knowing that, while I was safe in my egg, I wasn't feeling fulfilled.

Since I could not put my finger on exactly what was happening to me, I did not try to break free for quite a while. But the more things stayed the same, the more I felt the growing need for something to break up the monotony. Actually, I began to feel stranded inside a world in which I had once been so free!

What do *you* do when you are feeling stuck? I am sure that quite a few folks have had this feeling on the road to success, and they may offer several different roadmaps for getting loose. But, in hindsight, there were a few things that I did (and still do) when I realized that it was time for me to hatch. Following are my suggestions:

- *Accept and acknowledge where you are, so you are able to move forward.* Feeling stuck does not feel good. It is even slightly embarrassing to admit, because, doesn't everyone want to appear like they have it all together? But the truth is, we all feel stuck at some point in our lives. Understanding and accepting that reality will help you get unstuck.

- *Feeling stuck is internal.* It is your perception…and what I love about perception is that, when you change how you see things, things begin to change. You have to take responsibility for your life.

- *Become still.* Consider all that you are dealing with and what you have a desire to do. You may come to a point where you realize that your life is about to change, perhaps dramatically. During a hatching stage, we have to find time to be still and listen to our inner selves. There's a transformation happening. Your frustration of immobilization is part of the opening to freedom.

- *Prepare to choose wisely; do not rush.* In this time of searching your inner self, you are on the way to deciding what comes next. There were a lot of moments when I sat and stared at my journal, simply considering the possibilities of what could be missing from my life and what was going on inside of my head. I was not sure what was I looking for, so I could not be in a rush, even though I did not like living with the feeling of uncertainty.

- *It is not just about you.* Realize that when hatching happens and urges you to press forward, it is not just about personal gain. It is because a greater need is being fulfilled through you. True fulfillment is connected to something bigger than you.

As I was going through all of these feelings and inward journeys, I felt like a baby bird stuck at the bottom of my shell. I felt so many different emotions. As comfortable as I was with my assured A-list of clients, there was something inside me itching to come out. I decided I needed to break away from fundraising full-time to give space to my creativity, passions, and dreams.

What would hatching be like for you? What makes you feel the need to break away? If you allowed yourself to leave your place of comfort to get the life of fulfillment that most of us seek, what would you be doing? What is stopping you from moving in that direction? The honest answer may be that you are doing what you have to because you do not see the path to get to your passion project. Hatching is taking the first step of believing that you can and should pursue your passions.

I remember talking to my sister-friend Patrice Greer about this unusual and very uncomfortable time in my life. My life ambitions seemed perfectly normal to her, but I told her I felt dark and empty inside, with thoughts that were nearly crippling me. A few days later, she sent me a song by India Arie called "Break the Shell." I could not believe it—India was singing the words and describing exactly what I needed to set myself free. I must have listened to the song fifty times that day alone. It became my anthem for the next year of my life.

Although the process of hatching is one that can be scary, it is also liberating and completely fulfilling. As I listened to the words of that song, I realized that I had forgotten who I was. On paper, it looked like I knew myself, and I even believed it most of the time, but, as I began hatching, it was clear that I had forgotten the me of the moment. How can you begin to understand who you were meant to be when you have forgotten who you are? During the ongoing hatching process, I wondered if things would have been different or better if I had not made certain mistakes or experienced a tart, lemon-filled life before learning how to make lemonade. Living afraid of feeling hurt or failing was not going to be my path any longer. I had to take my chances and hatch.

When you have grown to full term inside your shell, the space that was once a just-right fit becomes tight and uncomfortable. Hatching provides not only new opportunities, but also newfound freedom to expand to your next level. Then there is your new viewpoint that comes with hatching. At the moment you decide to break free from who you were and hatch, a new light appears as your shell's surface is cracked wide open. The light shines a path for you to go that way, try this option, explore, grow, do, be! I know hatching is easier said than done. Trust me, it took nearly twenty years for me to take that first step. My advice for you is:

- *Do it scared.* The fear will disappear as soon as you make the first move.

- *Follow the breath of your heart.* Trust that you will grow into the person you feel, think, and believe you are in your heart and mind.

- *Do all things in love.* Love covers a multitude of sins. When you operate in love, fear and doubt are silenced.

- *Be present.* The best part of hatching is to be present. If you are able to spend less time worrying about your past or future, you could assess your current shell and crack it wide open.

The more you understand, the better a position you will be in to open up and begin the process of hatching. I think the greatest lesson is to understand that you can learn so much about your personal hatch experiences through close observation. Breaking out of a shell initially can be shocking. But remember, this place is new and unfamiliar, so it is critically important for you to be fully aware of your surroundings before exposing yourself to the elements and vultures waiting on the sidelines. They often have a nose for vulnerability and frailty.

Hatching is the beginning of something uncomfortable at first, but beautiful in its time. This is why part of hatching is to understand the type of behavior you need to replicate to ensure that your breakthrough process is protected and nurtured. How you behave and respond to your needs and weaknesses during a hatching period can be the deciding factor in your future ability to soar or stay down, like a grounded bird.

Chapter Two

Becoming

"For me, becoming isn't about arriving somewhere or achieving a certain aim. I see it instead as forward motion, a means of evolving, a way to reach continuously toward a better self. The journey does not end."

—Michelle Obama, *Becoming*

I t was such an incredible experience to sit and listen to the wisdom First Lady Michelle Obama poured out as she spoke to a packed audience during her *Becoming* book tour. What was most impactful was the fact that this beautiful, accomplished, and respected woman (who is also a graduate of Princeton and Harvard) was so transparent about her journey that was far from perfection and forever evolving.

It was widely reported that Michelle's superpower during her book tour was her ability to create intimacy at a large scale; specifically, at arenas, with seating capacities hovering around twenty thousand. She was not always able to share her feelings like that. In fact, she told reporters that, during her time as First Lady, she felt obligated not to let the country see her vulnerabilities. She felt that her job was not to nurture herself. But when she and Barack left the White House, she was ready to hatch, leap, and soar.

She was able to write and share her feelings in *Becoming* about her personal journey, including the fertility treatments she received, the miscarriages she endured, and the marriage counseling the couple went through after their children were born. It just goes to show that even the most highly regarded individuals are often going through the same feelings you have. Amazing, but true.

When she was First Lady, there was a tremendous amount of pressure that was unduly and often subconsciously placed on Michelle to *arrive* at a particular place or position in order to be validated. I agree wholeheartedly with her clear sentiment that the true measure of validity should be seen as the ability to keep arriving, arising, and evolving. The person who refuses to stay stagnant for too long and seeks to constantly become a better version of themselves is the one who will enjoy the most fulfilling life.

While I did not feel a stroke of lightning at the initial moment that I faced moving out of my comfort zone in order to hatch into a better version of me, I later realized that it was one of the highlights of my life. In *becoming,* you actually acknowledge that, to get to the best version of yourself, there will be fears to face, hurdles to overcome, and a perpetual process of starting again to evolve into the best that you can be.

After spending several seasons of my life securely fixed in what I thought was a safe place, I now enjoy a newfound freedom in the art of becoming. Like most things worth having, this process is beautiful in the end, but is most definitely a process. Becoming is also a personal commitment to taking the necessary steps to reach your place of awakening.

Over the span of my fundraising career, I raised more than fifty million dollars. I had become a prolific and sought-after fundraiser. But at the same time, a quiet disruption was happening inside me that seemed to be urging me to stop and examine "who was I created to *be*" versus "what I was good at *doing*."

I distinctly remember the series of events that began to push and provoke me to dig deeper into those thoughts. I had accepted a volunteer role as children's director for my church. It was an absolute dream. I loved helping children learn and develop a relationship with Jesus. I also enjoyed providing motivation and support to their parents. Once again, I felt that I was doing what I was created to do.

Even though I also had a full-time job, working as a volunteer was what centered me. I felt as if I was living a fulfilled life. With fulfillment comes fruitfulness, which was reflected in the community's growth. I was not the only one who I could see what was happening in the children's ministry. My pastor decided to offer me a full-time *paid* position as the children's director. I was overjoyed! It felt so right! And, while it would turn out to be a huge pay cut, my husband and I discussed it and agreed that it was an opportunity that I should pursue.

I was convinced that this was the right path for me. I was willing to pare down our spending and go without the things that did not really matter to become who I was meant to be. There is something exhilarating about peeling back the layers of excess to reveal the number of objects holding you back. Without these encumbrances, you can get back to the core desires of your heart and become you again.

I submitted my resume and waited.

A few short days later, I received a call from the church's human resources department to book my first interview, which would be over the phone. When I joined the call that day, I found that I was interviewing for an entirely different position. If this chain of events surprises you, consider how I felt!

While the interviewer assured me that I would remain as the volunteer children's director, he then offered me a position as director of sponsorships and fund development, which came with a very healthy salary.

Even though this was a different outcome than what I had expected, at the time it seemed to make sense. After all, wasn't I really good at raising money? So, it was a *logical* fit. Right? Wrong!

The problem was that I had planned an order of operations for myself, and this new state of affairs was not part of my strategy. In retrospect, I realized that, during this particular season of my life, I was beginning to hatch out of what I was good at and break into what I was created to do. Unfortunately, I did not take hatching into consideration when weighing the pros and cons of this offer. Needless to say, I took the job.

While it was an amazing opportunity and I excelled in my role, I once again found myself back in the same rut I had been trying to escape. I was feeling unfulfilled. As if that was not enough, because the position was extremely demanding, it was not long before I had to resign from my volunteer role with the children's ministry. Even now, when I think about this turn of events, I sigh out loud. Because I was unable to invest the needed time and effort into what I believed the children and their parents deserved, I let it go.

This was such a conflicted time for me. Working with the children—motivating and inspiring them—was the place where I had felt the most joy. But I had to give it up for more time to work in a job that I was "good" at. I was right back where I had been before. This turned out to be a *huge* setback to my hatching process.

Once again, I began to feel the tightness of an invisible shell around me that I desperately needed to break through. Once again, I realized that my comfortable place was anything but. I just *had* to hatch.

Looking back at those feelings, I understand now that the process of breaking through your own personal shell can take the form of many obstacles. My fundraising abilities were just one thing keeping me from breaking free.

I am here to tell you that the process of breaking free is no picnic.

- It is scary.

- It is tiresome.

- It is difficult...but in the end, it is definitely worth it!

The primary reason that breaking through and breaking out takes so much effort is because finding out who you are created to be does not always feel good. It is not easy to reevaluate yourself. But, one of the most fascinating exercises that I have ever done is to look into my own psyche. I vividly remember the erratic emotions that erupted as I hit this unfamiliar place in my process. The feeling I remember most was vulnerability.

I had grown through the ranks to become a master at fundraising. Did breaking out of my shell mean that all the knowledge I had acquired over the years would be for nothing? An even greater concern was that I might have to make my way through the ranks of a completely new area of expertise.

The answer was yes and no. No, because my fundraising skills would become essential tools to help me build my personal brand. And yes, I would have to grow and learn additional skills while transitioning into my next role. Although I was intrigued about what I *could* become, I was much more uncertain of what that role might be.

> *"Your talent is bigger than a profession. Your talent was given for a purpose. Use your talent for the purpose for which you've been put on the planet."*
>
> —Dr. Steve Perry

When you are in pursuit of your purpose, or if you are deciding whether you should follow your dreams, the pathway forward may seem questionable. Many questions will run through your head. *Is it the right decision? What could go wrong? What will happen if everything goes right?* I asked myself all of these questions, and sometimes I still do. These are the times when you should really dig deep, find your self-confidence, and take the advice of motivational speaker Lisa Nichols. I had the opportunity to attend the Disney Dreamer Academy as a member of the press and sit in on a session with Lisa. This was my third time hearing Lisa live at a Disney Dreamer Academy, but on Friday, March 9, 2018, she changed my life.

I am not sure if it was her pure genius, my thirst for knowledge and growth, or the timing of my life. I was ready to take a risk and believe in my own magic. Lisa's amazing story begins when she was a single mom on public assistance with twelve dollars in her bank account and a baby wrapped in a towel (instead of a diaper). She had hit rock bottom. She struggled trying to care for herself and her son.

Then she had a shift and today, more than twenty years later, she is a millionaire entrepreneur, a best-selling author, a humanitarian, and a motivational speaker. It felt like she was speaking directly to me when she said, "Bet on You!" It was at that moment that she aroused a sleeping giant within me. As she stood there, bold, radical, powerful, and passionate, I could not help but hang on every word as tears streamed down my face. I finally felt that I deserved to give myself permission to *Bet on Me*!

You can have the same epiphany. You have to bet on yourself before anyone else does. Believe in the fact that all of the essential elements you need are already inside of you. Believe that you can and will succeed in accomplishing even more than you have ever dreamt about. This journey of living out your dreams is like relying on an internal GPS tracker. Trust that, even if you have to recalibrate, your navigational system will always safely guide you to your destination.

As you venture toward that passion, remember that, even if you take a wrong turn, you have what is needed inside you to get to your personal place of fulfillment. The most important action you will take is to engage yourself in this process.

As difficult as your journey may become, you cannot worry about what others think about your actions. Only you can decide if your decisions are right or wrong. Reserve that power for yourself. And trust yourself! Give yourself permission to change direction. If it is not what you originally planned, so what? Life is all about change, and taking a new route is your choice to make.

"You miss 100 percent of the shots you do not take."

—Wayne Gretzky

When you begin to reevaluate and discover yourself on the pathway to purpose, expect a definite learning curve. This process is not always comfortable or uncomplicated. But there is a simple way to become more at ease with your possible missteps and new learnings. Open yourself up to the vulnerabilities of not knowing where you might land. This is especially true if you have been at an expert level for many years in a totally different area. If you learned how to excel once, you have the potential to learn again. Imagine how you will thrive and achieve that much more once you tap into who you were created to be!

I bet you want to reach out to ask me, "Is there one specific thing that I should do to become who I was created to be? If so, how do I find it?"

To be honest, there is no one, cookie-cutter answer to figuring out exactly what you will do or who you will be next. Remember that hatching is about removing restrictions. In this process, you can and *should* explore new opportunities as they come to you.

For example, I remember the first time my friend Vickisa invited me to a Bikram Yoga class. Initially, I did not know if I should be insulted or inspired. When someone is insecure, she (meaning me) might easily misinterpret an innocent remark. I took the high road and initially thought doing yoga seemed easy, but the heat factor gave me serious pause. I thought, *You mean to tell me that we are in one room for 90 minutes, in 105-degree heat, at 40 percent humidity, and doing the same 26 postures in every class?* The class did not sound like something I would voluntarily sign up for. "Oh, okay girl," I said to Vickisa in my sarcastic voice.

A few days later, I walked into that same Bikram Yoga studio with a plastic water bottle, a rented mat, and no idea what I had gotten myself into. But surprises never cease! I used my thirty-nine-dollar trial pass several times over the next few weeks and, once my trial ended, I found myself subscribing to a monthly plan. I ended up attending classes four to five days a week. I *still* practice Bikram Yoga so many years later. I have made significant progress in my practice, even though I still cannot do some of the harder poses. I keep on trying. Who would have thought that I would become a yogi and that my journey would teach me so much about myself and the benefits that yoga added to my life? *In this instance, I certainly hatched!*

The most important lesson of hatching is to embrace the process. Break out mentally, emotionally, and spiritually for each new level of growth, development, and maturity that you reach. Then go ahead and do it all over again.

Let's revisit the image of the unhatched baby bird. In the baby bird's beginning stage, it is equipped for formation inside of the egg. However, once the baby bird reaches full term, it hatches from that same egg into a season where it learns to function outside its shell. The bird continues to evolve, one level at a time. Its purpose includes learning how to fly; at another level, it will become impregnated; and in yet another level, it will reproduce. If it stays within the shell's confines, it will probably become inert.

The same is true for you as one of God's greatest creations. There are inherent stages of development and markers of growth that you progressively met as you matured. For example, as a newborn infant, crying was the only form of communication that you had to share your needs with your parents. But there was a point at which you evolved and learned how to communicate with single words, then sentences. You forged ahead from kindergarten through higher education, so there is no reason to stop progressing to the next level now!

Every season will bring you new stages of development, new personal assignments to fulfill, and new seeds to nurture. Unless you continuously hatch into your next season, you will risk *going bad* in the last environment you have outgrown. Why is there such a risk attached to staying the same? And what does it really mean to *go bad*?

With the 20/20 vision of hindsight, I can clearly answer that question with some of the feelings that started going bad in me.

- The longer I remained inside my shell, the more frustrated I became.

- The more I realized that I should be doing something different with my life, the more I realized I was conforming to the expectations of others.

- I found myself becoming insecure where I had once been confident.

- I started seeing behaviors in myself that showed me I was becoming the type of person I had always despised.

- The longer I stayed comfortable within my shell, the more uncomfortable I became. I was "going bad."

It is easy to miss the potential of your *now* by staying still in the comfort of the present with your pains of the past or your fears about the future. If you were to stop and honestly assess yourself and your life today, are there any instances that do not feel right emotionally, mentally, spiritually or physically? Can you name what they are? Do you know where these feelings stem from? It could be just one strong, incessant issue or a multitude of contentions that you've hidden away in your shell.

Faith is the one essential element that you need to hatch. The answer is to find faith in yourself. Right now! Today! You do not have to be religious to have faith. The definition of spirituality, which is a "strong belief in God or in the doctrines of a religion," need not apply when hatching. I am simply suggesting that you put your complete trust or confidence in *something*!

In the early 2000's, When I took the leap to join the staff at St. Philip's, not only did I take a pay cut, I took the opportunity to take a chance. In the past I had raised money and resources for events, and I was even awarded for raising the most money for a Multiple Sclerosis Bike Ride while working a full-time job. But taking on a full-time development job, where I was responsible for raising $1.5 million a year, was indeed a leap and a true act of faith.

Your commitment to asking, seeking, and trusting the lead of your higher power will become the demonstration of your faith. You may not be a person of faith, so let me put it to you this way: when you have faith no matter what happens, you will not fail. Why? Because having faith means that you've still won. You trusted yourself enough to try, and, in that exercise, you learned something about who you are.

Hatching to flee from a redundant and mundane lifestyle is an innate desire. Deep down inside each of us is the overwhelming need to use our gifts, talents, and abilities to do something extraordinary. Just think—your actions may lead to personal profits or growth or add value to the world in which you live. A unique and full-circle sense of completeness may emerge when you use what is inside of you to uplift or help others who have not yet been able to hatch themselves.

Hatching with the hope of fulfillment is easier to understand than saying, "I broke through the ceiling" because I was unfulfilled in my previous environment, career, or life. Seeking fulfillment is a journey to reconcile your outer life with an inner understanding of how to reach your full potential. You should use your inner powers on purpose. It is like having a deep, internal itch that must be scratched! Fulfillment is experienced when you can look at your work and know that it mattered. It is encountered when you are able to observe the full and final process of what you strived for finally achieved.

The Purpose Driven Life: What on Earth Am I Here For?, a book written by Pastor Rick Warren, became a popular banner, leading individuals to seek out their own purpose in a deep and meaningful way. Rick is often called "America's most influential spiritual leader." This best-selling book in the Religion and Spirituality category has helped millions of readers examine how to achieve a place in life that was inspired and live according to what was purposeful.

How do *you* find and follow the clues to find purpose? Listen to your inner voice that is urging you to spread out and grow. Move toward the ideas that motivate and inspire you. Take a step beyond your comfy, complacent space, and hatch into a place that requires more of you. Flourish into the next and best version of yourself, again and again.

You will find that your journey is constant and ever-evolving, moving into varying levels of self-encouragement, such as saying to yourself, *I should do this. I can do this!* You will learn how to confidently do what you were created to do and fulfill your purpose. Sounds exciting, does it not?

The flip side of fulfillment is that it is never just about you. When you begin to fulfill your purpose, it also becomes an answer to the need of another. Your new business or nonprofit idea will provide a solution to a problem that you were most driven by and passionate about. The way you are evolving as a student, leader, spouse, parent, and more will ultimately benefit the lives of those who you are connected to. When you examine yourself and conclude that you have used your skills and abilities unselfishly for the benefit of others, you will experience what it means to be fulfilled!

Who were you created to be? How will you hatch and begin your process of becoming? I personally have decided that I will not walk in the shadow of what I do best. I will not abandon who I am purposed to become. I invite you to join me on this journey by reviewing the following:

- Review your current role in life and ask yourself the question, *Is this who I was created to be?*

- Using your new, fresh perspective, write down three actions that you will take to begin your process of *becoming.*

Relax and relieve yourself of the pressure and anxiety of *perfection* or *having arrived*, and allow yourself to simply hatch and *become.* I may make it sound easy, and, trust me, it truly is. Honestly speaking, for most of my life, I made things way too hard for myself. I hindered my own ability to fully *become* because I was way too busy trying, and most times, pretending to be perfect. But sooner or later you will realize, as I did, that *becoming* is an inward journey. This process of self-discovery entails learning new insights about yourself that will eventually help you define who you want to be. Becoming is a process of self-development: working and taking the steps to transform yourself. Finally, to become is a process of self-acceptance, which is loving the person you are right now, even if you never change. Only then will you gain the power to hatch and become.

By giving yourself permission to discover your true self and align your life's journey around your core beliefs, values, and perspectives, you will uncover the things that will bring you total fulfillment.

Chapter Three

Your Potential

"We'll never know our full potential unless we push ourselves to find it."

—*Travis Rice*

Have you ever looked at a person and said, "Man, they sure have a lot of potential?" What did you mean? What did you see in that individual? Did you catch a glimpse of what he or she could achieve or how well they could accomplish a specific task with just a little effort?

I am convinced that the potential to be and to do more exists inside each and every one of us. As you commit to doing what it takes to obtain success, internally or externally, you also commit to doing what is necessary to maximize your potential.

As its definition states, the word *potential* means untapped qualities that may be developed and lead to future success. The question then becomes, *Why are those qualities untapped?* The easy answer is that your own qualities lie deep inside you, unknown or undiscovered. But that may be only part of the equation. The other part rests in your willingness to push yourself to find what lies deep within. I know firsthand that we all receive clues and urges to tap into what is already inside of each of us. The ability to do more is buried within.

I have personally seen those clues come in the form of passion about a certain matter, a unique way of accomplishing tasks or reaching people, and a desire to learn about a particular subject matter. Often, your interests or passions may not be in the more comfortable areas where you work, serve, or perform. However, if you do not put yourself in vulnerable or uncomfortable situations, you will never know exactly how much potential resides within you. Each of us has been uniquely made with purpose. You have been equipped to reach great levels of fulfillment. If you take a moment to stretch and push yourself to new limits, you will find the latent potential hidden deep inside.

When I was a little girl, my grandmother would often tell me she believed in me and that I could achieve whatever I put my mind to. If I worked hard, I could make it happen. She did not have one doubt because she saw the potential that I had inside. That's why I can tell that **you** were created for greatness.

Let's face it…looking inside and seeing your greatness within is often difficult. It was for me. Not only are we our own worst critics, there will always be certain people who will try to crush us with their words. *You're not good enough. You will never amount to anything.* Those negative voices can often become ingrained in our beliefs, cloud our vision, and make us doubt ourselves. Words have power. They can cut deep, or they can heal and empower. The words we choose when speaking to ourselves and others can make all the difference in the world.

Some people may think that I have it all together because I wrote a book or have a business. I even get to experience some amazing once-in-a-lifetime events for my job as a blogger. But the truth is, I am constantly questioning my abilities and, more importantly, my impact. I do not always feel adequate, qualified, stable, or inspiring. As a matter of fact, most days I feel average. Why? Because I have experienced close friends speaking against my decisions and my personal truths. At the time, I thought their words could ruin my life, but looking back, I know I was being slightly dramatic. Even so, I wanted to strive for perfection so that they would say more positive and affirming words to me.

My grandmother Shirley raised me from a young age because my mother intermittently moved in and out of my life. I lived in the same house as numerous aunts and uncles who essentially all played a role in raising me. I remember one of my aunts telling me that my grandmother spoiled me. She was right. My grandmother absolutely spoiled me, mainly because she wanted me to be aware of her love.

One day, my aunt decided to speak out about what I imagine was on her mind for a very long time. I was just a small child, but I remember that moment as if it was yesterday. Something must have happened to make her snap. She stood up, glared down at me, and said in no uncertain terms, "You'll never be anything. You'll never be anything because Shirley has spoiled you." I'm not sure why my aunt said those things to me, but she was dead wrong. The funny thing is, I never allowed what she said to me that day to take away from the love and admiration

I had for her. But I never forgot what she said to me or the way those words made me feel.

As much as her words hurt, even as a child, I chose not to be defined by them. What I did not know then is that I could choose to live a life of purpose each and every day. I now understand that I am not defined by the situation into which I was born or by what any person has said to me.

I have made plenty of mistakes along the way, which sometimes negatively impacted my thought process. It was often challenging for me to see my own potential. Now, I am pursuing a passion, my purpose, and a calling to ensure that other people know the importance of how adults speak to children. No one should speak to our kids in a way that will cause them self-doubt.

Take the pledge with me now: "I will not speak ill about myself or my children. I will not live a life where I do not feel productive. I do not have to live that way."

Because of my imperfect childhood, my faith in God that he created me for the purpose of helping others, and a million other reasons, my husband and I founded a nonprofit organization, A Chance to Learn.

This organization was created because of my son Chance and is literally a labor of love. While trying to conceive a child with my husband Andre, I suffered several successive miscarriages before finally giving birth to my miracle baby. We named our son Chance because we believed God had given him a "chance" at life.

Chance was precocious, already reading around the age of sixteen months. He keeps me on my toes and in alignment with my purpose as his mom. When Chance was just two years old, we flew to visit members of our family, and he told me about a cousin who was also two but could not read. I explained that not every two-year-old can read, and not everyone can afford to send their child to daycare and preschool. Chance responded, "Well, I think you and Daddy should pay for every kid to go to preschool, because if they cannot read, then they cannot read their Bible." From the mouths of babes, right?

As soon as we got off the plane, I shared Chance's conversation with my husband, and a week later I filed the paperwork to start A Chance to Learn. The organization was created to combat the issue of children entering kindergarten who are behind the rest of the students. We focus on building skills that are important for children who are zero to five years old. As an advocate for early childhood education, we partner with daycare providers by providing courses of study. We also hold eight-week summer camps for children between the ages of three and five, focusing on academics and related extracurricular activities that will prepare them for kindergarten. Chance helped me to fulfill my life's purpose. Had we not started A Chance to Learn, I might not have been the motivated mom I am today.

Like me, once you become honest with yourself, you will be able to focus on aligning your efforts with *your* values, rather than what other people perceive is the right thing for you to do.

I remember moving to Dallas from Atlanta in 2002, as an advertising executive for Upscale Magazine. I began meeting a great group of people who were doing some amazing things in the community. I actually stalked an agency that served youth to find an opportunity to volunteer.

Not long after I spoke at this agency's girls' retreat (you know that I made the right connections with the right people to get there), I became good friends with one of the employees. Together we launched a program that I would end up taking to several cities in the US. Without even thinking about fear or intimidation, I went on a quest to solicit support for our newly named Girls' Night Out program.

I ended up getting several huge donations from Gillette, now part of Procter & Gamble. We were amazed at the number of donations that poured into the office for our one-night event. When the event launched, it was an overwhelming success. Nearly two hundred girls attended, dozens of volunteers helped, and I never once thought that I did not have what it took to host this event.

A short time later, I applied for a part-time position to run a mentoring program for St. Philip's School and Community Center. I remember meeting with Froswa Booker-Drew, director of the center at the time. I was super excited about mentoring the girls from South Dallas. I knew that I was in my element. I felt purposed and excited.

Froswa explained that I would have to interview with the executive director, which I thought was a bit strange, since I was applying for a volunteer position. But since I wanted the opportunity to serve, I eagerly proceeded. That screening interview with the executive director Dr. Terry Flowers turned into a four-and-a-half-hour encounter that was filled with tears, laughter, and inspiration. In fact, the session ended only because I had an event to attend for my full-time job at Upscale Magazine. The time I spent with him was clearly the best interview of my life. Two weeks later, he called to offer me the development position at St. Philip's. Without hesitation, I said, "Yes."

While everything inside me knew this was the right move, it did not make any logical sense. Accepting this position meant that I would be taking a more than thirty-thousand-dollar salary cut. It added up to a fifty-thousand-dollar decrease if I included my year-end bonus. *What was I thinking?* Here is the real deal…I did not want to miss an opportunity that I knew deep in my heart would change my life completely.

It is safe to say that when you are in pursuit of your purpose, or if you are deciding whether you should follow your dreams, the pathway forward may seem questionable. Second-guessing yourself is inevitable.

But as you move ever closer toward your dream, remember that, even if you take a wrong turn, you have what's needed inside of you to get to your place of fulfillment.

The most important thing is that you are making the decisions for yourself. As difficult as the transition may be, you cannot worry about what others think is right or wrong. Reserve that right and power for yourself. And trust yourself! You should give yourself permission to change direction. So what if it is not the path you have always planned to take? Do not deny yourself access to your wants and desires. It is worth it. I know because I did it!

After I accepted the position at St. Philip's, my experience was indeed life-changing. I decided to go back to school, then continued to get an advanced degree with a concentration in nonprofit management. I also became a volunteer at the Community Center and grew the girls' program from fourteen to nearly a hundred attendees.

Seeing who you already are inside and the amount of your own potential is a choice, and making that choice involves faith. Like anything else worthwhile in life, it is not easy. You have to be up to the challenge of trusting that you can do it.

I rely on the faith I have in myself and my faith in God to guide me. My feeling is that you just have to believe in something, and that could be yourself or whatever it is that moves you. You may have an inner voice or talk to yourself in the mirror—come on, we all do it!

Over and over again, I have an internal discussion with myself. "Listen to me. You overcome by the power of your own strength. Share what you've been through, because there's somebody else who needs to hear what you have done so they can have the power and the courage to face what they're dealing with. Do not be afraid. You do not have to ask for permission anymore. You have the authority to be who you were created to be because of the desires in your heart."

Changing the patterns of your life is an ongoing journey. Even now, as I continue to share my testimony, I will always honestly admit that I am a work in progress. With all you have to do every day—whether it is managing family, a job, your brand, your social media presence, or the tremendous desire to live a life of purpose—when do you have time to fully examine who your true self is?

Personally, I have not had much time to think about it. I actually choose to believe that I am the *perfectly imperfect* person in my head. I certainly do not proclaim to know it all, but I am confident in myself. I never think that I am everyone's favorite, but I am very likable. I do not consider myself a liar, but I am not always truthful. These are the feelings that I contend with. I am being honest about who I am and who I desire to be. One of the hardest things I've ever done is to be honest with myself. I know that sounds ridiculous, but it is true.

Early in my blogging career, I hired a blog coach, who turned out to be so much more. Not long after getting started, I admitted to her that I was hiding my truths. When she asked why, I revealed that I was afraid that people would judge me. But then she made a statement that has stayed with me until this very moment... "Well, then the real concern is, if you are hiding that truth, what else are you hiding?"

My heart nearly stopped as I tried to hide the panic on my face. This question shook me to my core. It made me think about all of the personal challenges I still have to deal with while pursuing a life of purpose. I definitely have a few more layers to peel back before I can fully understand how to get to the heart of who I was created to be. So far, I have come to understand that I hid because...

- I am sometimes afraid of success.

- I am not always confident in my ability to succeed.

- I am not the person I was before; sometimes I am afraid to let people see the real me.

What does hiding *my* truths have to do with you? Honestly, *my* actions have *nothing* to do with you, but the truths you are hiding from the world have *everything* to do with you. What has to happen for you to decide to let go of what has happened to you in the past to find total fulfillment, real success, and true happiness?

I will be honest with you; until recently, I was not okay with who I was. I did not have faith in myself. Growing up, I endured trauma, heartache, and the trials of being a member of a completely dysfunctional family. At times, it has been difficult for me to appreciate all the good that has come to me, despite the severity of all the bad. It is not easy for me to put my story into words without feeling like I am writing the script of a Lifetime movie. My past is not a pretty picture by any means, but it is important that I share my beginnings with you.

I grew up with two dads, like many children of broken families. Both were known in the local community as decent guys. What the folks in the community and I did not know was that my mother was raped by one of them when she was barely in her teens. The other took advantage of her as well.

To make matters worse, I was born as a result of my mother's rape. She never married either man; in fact, my first dad was already married when he attacked my mom. His friend, my other dad, decided to take some responsibility for me. While they both helped out and sent a few dollars here and there, they did little to make my mom's life easier. Throughout the years, I visited them both occasionally, but neither one of them was consistently present in my life.

As I grew up from a child to a teen, my life began to get even more complicated. I, too, was raped in my early teens, approximately the same age as when my mom was assaulted. I grew up thinking that men only wanted me for sex. I walked around as a wounded and scared little girl. I mostly kept these secrets, telling just a few friends over the years. In the second semester of my freshman year in high school, I tried living with my first dad. I'm pretty sure I was a handful. I had a lot to process in my undeveloped little mind and had no help, just condemnation from family and friends. I remember when both dads showed up at LaSonia's home while I lived with her. At that point, I was too hurt and depressed to even to care what these two "father figures" had to say. I don't even remember the content discussed during the conversation.

In retrospect, I was lucky that they were not around to cause me more pain or so I thought. During my young adulthood, I actually began to build a stronger relationship with my first dad; I never saw or spoke to the other. To be honest, it was really nice to have a dad present in my life—that is, until someone told me that he had raped my mom. Now I have a "some what" relationship with both of them. If I'm honest, and I am, I will tell you that had I had a solid relationship with both or either of my dads, I probably would have avoided a lot of hurt, pain, and emptiness from their lack of love and quality time.

The new pain I had to endure made it an extremely difficult time in my life. Imagine trusting the one person who had taken so much away from my family! But more importantly, I started questioning what the impact of being raped had on my mom and me. How would our lives have been different if we had never experienced rape? Neither one of us received any counseling in the aftermath. Maybe we both would not have lived our lives in so much pain. Maybe she could have been the kind of mother I always wished she would be; the kind who did not leave. But I was raised by a grandmother who sowed promise in my heart that I was worthy of love.

And, believe it or not, I considered myself lucky, because total strangers took me in and called me family. So, while I have one biological mother, I call several women who have come to my rescue "mom." I was introduced to LaSonia Lurry during the summer before my sophomore year in high school by my "other" dad's daughter, my sister Tonnja. LaSonia was a twenty-five-year-old woman with the heart to love and care for me. She invited me to be part of her family, and so I joined wholeheartedly.

LaSonia's brother Darin became my uncle, her mother Shirley became my grandmother, her aunts were my aunts and her cousins were my cousins…well, except for Cornell, because I thought he and I would end up married. Oh well, thankfully, the plans we make as teenagers do not always come true, but you get the point.

Sure, I spoke to my biological mom and my grandmother; I even visited them, but I lived with LaSonia. Through high school and my young adult life, I would have several more experiences like this. I am thankful and forever grateful for all of the mom-like models, like Jo Cooper, Michelle Williams (and her husband Leroy), and Loretta Dozier, who played a role in my life and who gave me such a rich understanding of what true motherhood was.

Somehow, through it all, I knew that I was greater than what I was born into. As a girl, I lived far too long in the shadows of my greatness, so when I "grew up," I fought like hell to live beyond my internal scars. *I* decided when it was time for me to live my life as I was created to live. How did I do it? I grew up understanding that my challenges made me who I was. They helped me persevere and become, well, more. I also embraced the idea that *It's okay not to be okay, but it's not okay to stay that way.* You do not have to be perfect in order to fulfill your purpose or make an impact.

The choices we make eventually make us who we are. Life's experiences shape us and could possibly ruin us, but they do not have to. I recently watched a movie (adapted from the novel by Jojo Moyes) that changed my life, my heart, and my way of thinking. Called *Me Before You*, it is a beautiful, romantic story of a mother's love, a man's determination to stay true to himself, and a woman's journey of learning how to love and live.

The movie's premise includes the twenty-six-year-old Louisa, a sheltered, small-town girl who helps her family financially by taking odd jobs, and Will, a young billionaire who was once a financial wizard and an extreme-sports ace. Of course, he is rich, good-looking and a tragic hero. Hey, I said it was fiction!

Will becomes a quadriplegic and permanently confined to a wheelchair after an auto accident. Will is initially resentful and bitter over losing his once-fantastical life. He also endures constant pain and finds little joy in living. His concerned mother hires Louisa to bring a ray of sunshine into his life. Soon they form a lovely friendship; she teaches him to enjoy life again, and he shows her how to be adventurous.

While viewing this bittersweet love story (I will not share the ending in case you are moved to watch it), so many thoughts ran through my head. The title, *Me Before You,* rang true to me.

- I thought of you and how much easier it would be to help you find your inner strengths without having to contend with my own self-truths.

- I thought of my son and how blessed I am to be his mother. But I also realized how important it is for me to take care of myself so that I can properly parent him.

- I thought of me before wedding my husband and how thankful I am to be with him today. I certainly do not want to lose any of the qualities that attracted him to me in the first place.

- I thought about my faith in a higher being, and how everything changed when I started believing. I do not want to ever go back to the person I was before.

Now I understand the guidelines by which I want to live. The woman I was before was the person who made me hide my truths. That version of me has been my biggest hurdle, and possibly my greatest enemy. She was the enemy in me.

At the end of the movie, Will writes to Louisa to explain many of his feelings, including that he hoped she would "live boldly and freely." That is *my* plan for living the rest of my life. I am living boldly and freely in my unique purpose. I challenge *you* to do the same.

It is absolutely true that we overcome our issues with our testimony. Becoming the best version of yourself is not easy. If you need to hire a coach, identify a companion who can help you find a ray of sunshine, or find an accountability partner, so be it. Share your story, find total fulfillment, and allow others to be set free by sharing theirs!

Here are a few thoughts to consider before you move on to your next chapter.

- Be honest with yourself about why and what you are hiding.

- Decide who you desire to be…then be it.

- Do not let the disappointments of your past determine your amazing future.

- Do not compare yourself to others. You do not have to do what everyone else is doing.

The potential of who you can become and what you can achieve is so vast. However, the key to reaching your potential lies in the ability to believe in yourself. Have no doubt in what you can accomplish. Believe that you are more than enough; you have everything you need to succeed. Doubt will paralyze your potential and steal your dreams. Author, pastor, and speaker on leadership John Maxwell said, "I have to know me to grow me." It is one of the truest statements I have ever heard. You are much more capable and remarkable than you give yourself credit for. You may not be able to see it right now, but there is amazing potential within you.

Do not let anyone else determine your success. If you do not consider it your duty to live up to your full potential, then you may live a life far short of what you desire and, more importantly, what you are capable of accomplishing.

Just realize that to get there, it takes a huge amount of effort, energy, and commitment. You create your own momentum.

Hatching = Total Fulfillment

"The voyage of discovery is not in seeking new landscapes but in having new eyes."

—Marcel Proust

I find such fulfillment as I hatch in different areas of my life. To me, hatching means that I have found another piece of my *why*, which is another term for purpose. The answer to your purpose, or your *why*, is found by breaking out of your shell to see all of the amazing possibilities available. Look inward at your own self to assess the innate qualities you possess. They will lead you on a road to the total fulfillment that lies within.

What are you doing to challenge yourself to grow or hatch?

_____

_____

_____

_____

_____

Who in your circle makes you smile and brings out the best in you?

_____

_____

_____

_____

_____

In which areas of your life do you see the biggest need or greatest potential to hatch?

_____

_____

_____

_____

_____

Of the three chapters, "Understanding," "Becoming," and "Potential," which one made you feel like you were ready to hatch, and why?

_____

_____

_____

_____

_____

Section Two

Leap

Chapter Four

Courage

"It takes courage to grow up and become who you really are."

—E. E. Cummings

I have learned that it takes courage to battle the untruths and the pain, mistakes, and shortcomings of my past. Courage is something that we all want. It is the ability to do something that you know is difficult or dangerous in order to get the outcome that you want. I believe your courage plays a huge role in how your life will develop from this point on. Think about fairy tales, Bible stories, or Hollywood screenplays you know that herald stories of bravery and self-sacrifice, which ultimately change the world for the good. Courage was the one thing the cowardly lion wanted most desperately in *The Wizard of Oz*. David mustered up the courage to battle Goliath in the Bible. The warrior and defender of Wakanda T'Challa displayed courage when he suited up to fight Killmonger and take his proper place on the throne in the movie *Black Panther*.

In every instance, courage played a role and even defined who these characters became. Still, courage is not just physical bravery; it is the absence of fear. And trust me, the absence of fear is a great thing. Fear will try to take over your mind and stop you from living up to your full potential. Living in fear could cause you to miss out on some amazing opportunities that would allow you to be the person that you've desired to be your whole life.

You might not follow your purpose or passion because you see yourself as inadequate or not good enough. You may struggle with the voices of past failures, epic letdowns, and personal insecurities. Your inner voice may say, *You will not be able to do it*, or ask, *What will people think?* You might have an underlying feeling that you do not deserve to be successful or happy. Have I struck a nerve yet? There are as many self-doubts that may prevent you from being who you were meant to be as there are reasons to break away from this type of negative thinking. It is not a question of whether you will succeed or fail, because everyone gains something positive from failing. I sincerely believe you have a purpose that is connected to your deepest passion. To take the first step, stop with the negativity and start believing in yourself.

I rang in the year 2015 with twelve months of hatching behind me and a world of possibilities ahead. I knew that I was different, but I also knew I was not yet done becoming the new me. And, just as clearly as the year before, a new word came to me for 2015—*leap!* I did not understand fully what that word meant for me or what my leap would be, but I was certain that it had everything to do with taking the necessary steps to get to my next level.

By definition, *leap* means "to spring free from; to pass abruptly from one state to another." As such, it is a leap that will actually get you to move out from the bottom of your shell and your comfort zone. Typically, when you think of a bird breaking free from its shell, the hatching starts at the top. Let's work on getting your shell broken so you can see the possibility that lies ahead in new and unfamiliar territory. The way that you go from *knowing* that there is a new world to actually *arriving* into that new world is the leap, and that takes courage!

Even though the leap is your next logical step, it can only come after you have made up your mind fully that you are better off outside of your self-imposed borders than you are immobilized within. Either you grow and leave behind the path of least resistance, or linger at this level indefinitely. Remaining in one place is not healthy for your psyche; it can cause a slow and painful death of your spirit. That description may sound dramatic, but in so many cases, it is true. Think about it—the womb is a place of creation and nurturing. If a baby stays there too long, it can become fatal for both the mother and the infant.

As you might have observed, leaping, just like the other levels, requires great effort, energy, and will. But more than anything, leaping requires internal confidence. I know that you can accomplish what you were created to do. But *you* have to believe and trust that you will succeed in a new self-determination.

Building your confidence and choosing to believe in yourself are essential steps to leaping and to achieving any type of success. Without confidence in yourself, the journey to see your own potential and move beyond questions of self-worth will be extremely difficult. For many different reasons, you will find that it is not uncommon to question who you are or what you are capable of achieving. Sadly, at times when you do not know the answers, it is so easy to begin filling that void with objects and people that are not in alignment with your dreams and goals. It is also easy to lose confidence in your purpose, talents, and ability to fulfill your destiny and to shrink back and settle for the safe space. But, as you build up belief in yourself and grow incrementally more confident, understanding that you *can* succeed will motivate you until you have actually accomplished what you set out to do! I often quote Walt Disney, who says, "When you believe in a thing, believe in it all the way, implicitly and unquestionable." That is the attitude you need to leap!

I believe in the magic of Disney and the magic that happens when I believe in myself! When you believe in the abilities within yourself, any self-imposed limitations will fall by the wayside. If your beliefs are the filters through which you can create your reality, what are your beliefs about yourself that will help you create the life you desire?

For me, it was about believing that I was no longer meant to work in a position of raising money to further the vision and ministry of others. Instead, it was time to allow my own ministry to flow out of me to help women, mothers, and entrepreneurs. In hindsight, I wish I had considered the Bible and counted the cost to commitment. In other words, all the so-called costs and all the so-called losses—everything—are nothing compared to the gains of having Jesus, the greatest treasure, in my life. The cost may be total in actual experience.

I understand now that you may have to do what you love while positioning yourself to do what you were created to do. Steve Jobs, cofounder of Apple Computer, once said, "The only way to do great work is to love what you do." I believe that, when we are passionate and love what we do, advancement is inevitable. Keep in mind that the type of leap I'm talking about will almost always come from within yourself and *not* from your employer.

> *"The only way to do great work is to love what you do."*
>
> —Steve Jobs

Leaping may take the form of a first step: enrolling in a new course, finishing graduate school, writing down the story of your life on the pages of your first book, pursuing your goal of becoming your own boss, or stepping up to accept a leadership role that you have rejected for so long.

For certain, the leap is about you shouldering the confidence to believe that you can do whatever you choose to do and using that newfound confidence to move toward your dream. It is about going toward what your conscience is calling you to. It is about obeying that inner voice that leads to inner peace.

The image of joyfully leaping into the place of your purpose and potential is a beautiful one. It is the happy ending that we all want, right? So why aren't we all leaping from one idea, one stage, or one step to the next?

Although the thought of leaping is promising and exciting, the process is not easy. Chances are that, in the moments before you leap, you will be faced with a mountain of reasons why it may not be the best idea.

For me, the days and moments that preceded my leap were when every self-doubt and excuse for *Why not?* began to emerge. Old bits and pieces of your past have a way of resurfacing just when it is time to leap. I am not talking about the old good stuff of dreams, but those deep-rooted negative words of discouragement, abandonment, abuse, or inadequacy. These ugly thoughts try their mightiest to derail your efforts just when you have decided to finally live a better life in spite of your past hurts.

I was working hard to meet the goals that others had set before me, and yet I knew that I was supposed to be working hard to birth and build the potential I had inside of me. I knew that I was supposed to relinquish the role others had formed for me. I knew I was supposed to quit my job and begin the motivational ministry that my conscience was calling me to do.

And yet, I stayed.

For every reason that I counted as motivation to go ahead and leap, two objections surfaced to entice me into thinking I was not ready and not sure. My self-doubts welled up as questions in my mind, like *Why in the world would I quit a job that I was good at, to do something that I was not sure about?* On the surface, I felt relatively certain the correct answer to my own question was *Stay put.* But deep inside, I wasn't sure.

Leaping has to happen from a place deep within. Because I was not sure, I needed to build up the faith I had in myself and my own power. I had to figure out the best way to find my inner strength.

> *"Growth is painful. Change is painful.*
> *But nothing is as painful as staying stuck*
> *somewhere you do not belong."*

—Mandy Hale

This was an extremely difficult process for me. It caused me to examine and stand face-to-face with how I portrayed myself to the outside versus who I was really feeling on the inside. Before I could gain the positive self-image that it would take to spring forward, I had to make a true assessment of what was causing me to doubt myself.

The term "growing pains" is literally the pain in the limbs and joints children feel during growth spurts. It might make you think about everything that a human body has to go through as it grows and transitions.

But what about the pain you feel when you are held back from unfolding, growing, and stretching into your next developmental level? It is real and distressing, even if you are the one holding yourself back! Leaping becomes a logical and relief-giving choice.

Looking back to a time when this was happening to me, I felt the conflict between change and resisting it. In the end, dealing with the pain of change was easier for me than the pain of resisting it. Ironically, I was at the height of my fundraising career, yet I was so uncertain about the value I was bringing to my employer at the time. In addition, the environment that I once found so fertile now seemed to be sullied and binding. In hindsight, I know that my self-doubt and questions of self-worth were precursors to the fact that it was time to leap.

It has been my experience that, when I do not obey the voice inside me, the result is that my internal struggle begins to show externally. I can feel my mood changing, and I become depressed. My attitude becomes less than joyful. And finally, my body tends to take the brunt of my discontent, and I become physically ill. The longer it took me to take the leap, the more I experienced health-related issues. When push came to shove, I had no choice but to make a change. I knew it was time to personally experience the quote from Charles Dickens, "The best way to lengthen out our days is to walk steadily and with a purpose."

> *"The best way to lengthen out our days is to walk steadily and with a purpose."*
>
> —Charles Dickens

But still, I bucked up against making the change…until I became terribly ill. Yes indeed, illness can be a tremendous eye opener. I was in my hotel room on a business trip, suffering from a headache that *Would. Not. Relent.* After canceling dinner with my family in the area, I took two over-the-counter pain relievers and lay down for a nap. The pain was so severe I could not sleep. Hours later, my left shoulder began to ache, and numbness traveled down my left arm. I remember jumping up and shaking my arm while thinking, *Something is really wrong here.* After trying to call my soundly sleeping husband, I went down to the front desk to get my rental car key. I told the front desk clerk that I needed my car to go to the hospital. Before I knew what was happening, the manager was on the other side of the desk with a blood pressure reader around my arm. After he took my blood pressure, he yelled out, "Call 911!" I was rushed to the hospital with stroke-level blood pressure of 189/170. I remember being in the ambulance and the medic looking at me with much fear. He later told me that he thought I was going to stroke out right in front of him. I was admitted immediately, treated, and later sent home for an extended medical leave.

After that experience, I realized that the more I resisted change in my life, the more unhappiness and illness became my reward. And the longer I stayed in the bondage of a job I did not love, the more constrained I felt.

So why deal with the pain of the fight? Why not just break free of the shell and put yourself into a new environment? Why not just quit the job you have come to despise and look for a new one? Why not act on the idea of starting your own business?

The answer at first is almost always, *What if?*

What if I fail? What if I start but cannot finish? What if? What if? What if?

Because leaping is such an exertion of effort, it will usually be predicated with a great amount of self-talk that starts out completely negative, then shakily, bit by bit, equals up to self-assuredness and confidence. On the road to self-discovery, begin taking down each internal roadblock that screams, *You cannot!* Have the courage to believe that you are valuable and capable, regardless of what you have been told in the past. Gather up the courage to leap. Face your inner roadblocks by screaming back at them, *I can!* In short, believe in yourself.

You are greater than all of the mistakes you have ever made, combined. Here are a few things to think about as you prepare to leap.

- Remove all doubt.
- Recite and repeat scriptures, words, or affirmations that can help counter your self-doubt.

- Remember past successes when you were courageous, and did it scared.

As you embark on the journey of embracing something new, there is a level of uncertainty and fear that can be anticipated with leaping into new territory. The thing about anticipation is that it allows you to prepare for what is to come. If courage is partly the absence of fear, then we must do what we can to remove fearful thoughts from our daily walk. As they present their arguments as to why you can't be successful, I encourage you to rebut them and redefine the terms. I have heard fear redefined with various acronyms, such as False Evidence Appearing Real or Face Everything And Rise. In both instances, we are in control of how we respond to the thoughts and feelings that come to rob us of courage. Let your self-talk build you up in courage, versus talking you out of it!

Chapter Five

Proper Positioning

"Positioning in pursuit of your purpose is critical to your success in life. Remember, great strikers are found in the proximity of the penalty box. That is strategic positioning."

—Oscar Bimpong

N o one has the intention to be unsuccessful. You may have doubted yourself every now and again, but you certainly do not intend to fail. However, I am not certain that we live in a manner that is conducive to being successful. By that I mean that, if you want to be successful in any area of your life, align your actions to bring success into your life. Making your passions profitable and positioning yourself for success does not take luck. You do not roll the dice and hope to have a successful business, a good year, or a fabulous life. Positioning is the thing that will help you align yourself to meet success. Proper positioning is asking yourself if your actions are aligned with the results you want.

I usually wait until the end of the year to determine if my results were in alignment with the goals that I set at the beginning of the year. I quickly learned that waiting until the end of the year gave me an opportunity to examine and correct my performance and strategies. I had to be honest with myself, and ask myself daily, *Will the actions I take today lead me to the results I want tomorrow?*

My daily actions to enhance my life include preparing my mind by deepening my knowledge and sharpening my skills. If you want to build your business, do you attend networking events to attract new clients? Do you sign up for conferences to broaden your knowledge? No matter where you are in your life, you need to expand your mind in order to position yourself for success.

My daily actions also included being accountable, being responsible, and making myself a priority in the choices I make. I had to decide how I was going to invest my time and energy each day to give me the maximum results. Are you the CEO of your life, or are you a franchise allowing others to make critical decisions for you? The most successful individuals are usually the hardest workers. They make a conscious decision to go the extra mile and do things others will not. Take a good look inward and ask yourself, *What are the actions I consistently take or the choices I make in order to enhance my life?*

Anyone who has had a measure of success would say that it was not a matter of chance, but rather a matter of consistent, conclusive choices. Of the hundreds of choices that you have to make each day, some leave you on top of the world, while others leave you flat in the dust. Often, it is just a matter of learning by trial and error.

Leaping is about taking a risk, so when you are ready, the act will probably not be trouble-free or straightforward. However, positioning yourself on the proper pathway is the best way to minimize the uncertainty involved. There are several positive actions you can take in order to best position yourself for success.

Many think that *positioning* is about getting close to people who have the ways and means to *hook you up* when it comes to your plans. While this route may provide a short-term solution, it is not what I believe the definition of positioning is in this case.

Instead, one of the smartest and best ways to ready yourself for a successful leap is by explaining to the person who you have identified as good counsel that you are an eager student who is teachable regarding even the most rudimentary ideas. Taking this position is not about diminishing what you already know; it is about being proactive and prepared to supplement your knowledge. It is all about understanding who you are and where you want to be. You are setting up a foundation for success and creating a plan that lets you soar.

There are so many small things to consider as you are gearing up and putting yourself in the right position. However, I believe that the pathway to achievement is paved with two essential elements: directional markers and connecting with the appropriate people.

"Take a deep breath. Get present in the moment and ask yourself what is important this very second."

—Greg McKeown, Essentialism

In planning your leap to your next level, first carefully consider what you want to achieve. How will you know when you have arrived? What will you need to be effective there? These questions serve as directional markers that outline the course you will follow to your new endeavor. The answers should provide you with the necessary tools, habits, and disciplines to get to your *there*.

Understanding *where* you want to go is not always easy, at least not for me. We all want to be successful, but success is a subjective term that means something different to each of us. The ways and means we measure it are also completely individual.

Some believe that achieving fame and fortune, like movie-star status, is their destiny (that may be reaching a bit, but if you do not try, you'll never know!). Others may decide that a healthy relationship is their top indicator. Still others would define success by the ranks they have climbed throughout their careers, getting a graduate degree, originating a new nonprofit organization, quitting smoking, or losing weight. The ideas for personal success are endless, and do not have to stop after you have achieved just one. But it is important to focus on one goal at a time so that you do not get lost in a flurry of numerous false starts.

Once you determine the definition of what success means to you at this moment in your life, you can then create directional markers to help get you there. The dictionary defines success as "the attainment of a desired outcome or aim." Do you want to know what excites me about that definition? It is right in line with what it means to be purposed, which by definition means to "to be aimed."

This is an important point to remember. When you achieve what you aim to do, you are walking in purpose. And when you attain that purpose, you are walking in true success! There are not enough words in the universe for me to explain to you how actually achieving my purpose has freed me. For so long, my success measure was how much money I raised or how well I was doing in the eyes of others. That line of thinking also made it difficult for me to understand how leaping toward a life of motivating and inspiring others was enough to be qualified (and quantified) as successful. Now I realize that achieving new heights was always part of my inner soul, so my potential for success was sure.

I have always had a soft spot in my heart for the underserved. I suppose that is why I fell in love with working in the nonprofit sector. In 2016, as I was deciding how I wanted to redefine my life and in the midst of launching Motivated Mom, I decided to take a trip to Lagos, Nigeria. I traveled there on behalf of the USAF Global Business Development organization (not affiliated with the US Air Force), which provides leadership, guidance, and techniques of success for business and education enhancement. The USAF Global Foundation afforded me the opportunity to speak at a Global Leadership Conference and take part in one of its programs that provided aid to local schools. The USAF Foundation's mission is to provide social/human services as well as education enhancement programs to underserved communities in the United States and Africa, while building better lives and communities.

I had never seen poverty on that level. But I was there, first and foremost, to make a difference. I was excited to help. Over the course of a week, I was engulfed by the people, the culture, and their plight. I worked as an extension of the foundation to provide programs and services in the areas of education, social services, and emergency relief to the locals. The schools lacked basic resources like running water and restrooms, not to mention books, supplies, and playgrounds. The more I saw, the more I wanted to help. The children's faces are forever ingrained in my mind: some smiling, others hurting, many struggling…but living nonetheless.

It was difficult to see the children squatting to use the restroom on the side of the school or their mothers walking miles to sell peanuts, windshield wipers, candy, or whatever they could purchase and resell to buy food to feed their families. I began to realize just how my transition was creating clarity for my path of purpose.

> *"What you do makes a difference, and you have to decide what kind of difference you want to make."*
>
> —Jane Goodall

Giving to others brings me great joy; it is tied to my DNA; it is how God made me. Giving of myself is what I love to do. I do not mean just material things; I love giving hope, inspiration, motivation, and opportunity to others.

Each day I stayed in Lagos, I learned and accepted more about myself; I had become more comfortable with who I was. The more I peeled back the layers, the more I understood why my transition was essential.

Everything you do should ultimately align with who you are and your purpose. Life is too short for anything else. Knowing why you were created is the second-best feeling in the world, next to doing what you were created to do.

Spending time in Nigeria helped get me closer to fulfilling my purpose. I returned with a clarity about my desire to continue encouraging moms to be great women and extraordinary. The trip also renewed my passion to advocate, promote, and advance early childhood learning through A Chance to Learn. I wanted to do this with all of my heart. I knew then that I *had* to choose to live a life of purpose. That meant I had to say yes to things that aligned with my beliefs and allowed me to be my most authentic self. I was on the way to positioning myself to soar!

It is time to measure your successes in a new way. Never stop asking yourself, *What are my ambitions? How can I achieve my goals? How many goals have I attained today?*

Success is intentional. It begins with a vision. Incrementally, that vision is achieved, through the process of time and action. By continually doing the internal and external work necessary, you will move in the right direction and position yourself for success.

Real success is measured by goals. For the total effect, here are several rules of thumb regarding your goals.

- Write them down. Use ink, pencil, a favorite-colored crayon, laptop or cell phone, as long as your thoughts are clearly stated.

- Keep goals practical, reasonable, and measurable; embrace ideas that you can act on, demonstrate or learn.

- Set a timetable and a deadline for yourself. If by chance you do not meet that timestamp, adjust and reset; do not give up with an easily said, "Forget it."

- Consider something out of your reach, but within your grasp. Your goal should connect to the bigger vision of your life.

A great vision is accomplished by a thousand steps, guided by meeting clearly focused goals. For example, in the mind of an architect, a high-rise office building first begins as a vision. She then transcribes that vision and gives the blueprint to a construction company that builds out the vision, one brick at a time.

The same is true for the places that we choose to leap toward, including the inspirations hidden deep inside you. They are yours for the taking and will impact the world greatly, as long as you move toward them with confidence in your heart and a goal-driven vision in your mind. And please remember to write down your thoughts, or you may lose them in the chaos of everyday life.

The next critical element of positioning yourself for success is surrounding yourself with the right people!

Even with a well-thought-out plan of where you want to go, seek out individuals to help you successfully get there. Perhaps the most difficult part of this process is admitting that you need help. But believe me when I say that everyone needs assistance, in one way or another, at some point in their lives. Once you understand the need for support, allow yourself to receive wise counsel from others. They may also serve as an accountability system to guard you against running into unnecessary pitfalls.

"What has been will be again, what has been done will be done again; there is nothing new under the sun."

—Ecclesiastes 1:9 KJV

In today's age of rapid answers, the abundance of information and unlimited access to knowledge, there is no reason you would seek to leap without some sort of initial insight. Especially when you consider that there is nothing new under the sun. I am sure Steve Jobs, Jonas Salk, and Thomas Edison would beg to differ, but in general, most ideas are regenerated from what others have developed.

It is a wonder why anyone would run the risk of leaping into new territory that has more than likely been mastered by someone else. Whether it is starting a business, forming a nonprofit, volunteering in the ministry field, or any other spark of an idea you might have, it is safe to say that you could seek and find a source of wise counsel. Take it from me; learn from others who have successfully mastered a similar feat.

Many of us are fortunate to have natural supporters in our corner who listen to our concerns, talk us through our logical and sometimes illogical thought processes, and provide encouragement along the way.

While having a cheering squad to back you is incredibly helpful, it is not the same as obtaining wise counsel. Individuals who have the merit to mentor or coach you will provide more than just a few encouraging words. Instead, they provide sound counsel that comes from years of experience. Their coaching will help you prepare for both the positive and negative issues that you may encounter. They know and can share specific strategies and insights to help you successfully navigate and prepare for possible pitfalls. With the right counsel, you will be well-prepared to move forward with your vision.

The idea for the Motivated Mom program and platform sprang from an encounter I had while teaching a parenting class. It was during a session of A Chance to Learn summer learning camp for kids. Many of the parents who enrolled their children in my summer learning camp were not very engaged in their children's education, at least from the district's perspective. The parents asked me to teach a class on parent engagement. At the end of the class, most of the moms told me, "It is hard to be engaged because I do not have this, or I am not that."

Many attendees were single mothers who lacked confidence in their parenting abilities, as well as in their personal lives. They simply did not feel like they were great moms. Shortly after leaving the class, I called a friend to tell her that it was one thing to advocate education, but I wanted to motivate this group to be great women and extraordinary moms. I wanted to provide them with hope, confidence, and knowledge, so that they would be able to raise their children without self-doubt. My friend was so excited that she shouted into the phone, "That's it! You should call yourself the Motivated Mom." And so that is what I became.

I started the Motivated Mom platform with a four-city tour. I really had no idea what to expect, but I was fueled by pure passion and a desire to help motivate moms. I received a commitment from a sponsor to help fund my dreams. I had planned a jam-packed day of seminars, keynote speakers, and networking. When I arrived at my first stop in Chicago, nearly 200 moms were in attendance. I knew of the 140 who had registered, but there were almost 60 walk-ins that day. They were so excited to be there! The event turned out to be fabulous. Of course, that is when the questions from the crowd began… "Where can I follow up?" "What's the name of your blog?" "Do you have a website?" "How can I get involved with your organization?" I was overwhelmed, surprised, happy, and terrified, all at once.

It was hilarious because I had not even thought about these additional channels of communication until then. I said to myself, *Okay, I guess I need a blog and a website.* I immediately hired a designer to build my site and launched my first blog post about four weeks later, as I continued to plan the next step of the tour.

While traveling for the tour, I realized that I needed to learn more about blogging, including the back end, search engine optimization (SEO), how to attract subscribers…you name it. So I began researching blog coaches in my area who could help me learn how to operate, understand, and grow my blog. I found Elayna Fernandez, whose moniker and website name is "The Positive Mom." I hired her immediately! *(Okay, we did have one consultation beforehand, but I loved her and could not wait to hire her!)*

Before my first session, Elayna asked me to take the passion test found on her website. I followed her instructions and submitted my completed pre-steps forty-eight hours before my appointment. The test required that I write ten statements that start with the phrase, "My life is ideal, and I am ___ing." She told me that each phrase referred to intentions and aspirations that I wanted to create in my life (as opposed to what I was actually living). I wrote down the most meaningful desires I held in my heart, even from my childhood. Elayna suggested I use what she dubbed her Ten Fs as a guide: Family, Faith, Friends, Fitness, Finances, Fun, Forever Partner, Funding, Fulfillment, and FIRST (taking care of yourself first).

After understanding what I wanted to do and why, she taught me how to enhance my writing and helped me rebuild my website and social media platforms to gain more traction. I also began following other bloggers and taking courses to broaden my knowledge and understanding.

Choya Porter is the diva who runs the *Just a Splash of Diva* blog, a place to learn how to save money while shopping your heart away. She was another blogger who shared so much knowledge and exposed me to many online tools and taught me how to use them. She suggested tools like:

- IFTTT (if this, then that), the easy (and free) way to get my apps and devices working together.

- Tweet Deck, a highly specialized service that offers Twitter users a comprehensive and free way to manage multiple Twitter accounts.

- CoSchedule, a sort of mission control for online marketers that proactively creates weekly schedules.

I could go on, but in essence, I sought to learn from people who already were crushing what I wanted to do.

After getting sound advice from field experts, attending several conferences, and learning as much as I could about blogging and acting as a brand ambassador through blogging and social media, I had the good fortune to receive a few opportunities to work with brands and to go on a few press trips. I thought, *Okay, I am ready to do this!* That's when I decided to leap to begin working full-time on the Motivated Mom platform. Boy oh boy, that became a much more difficult leap than I ever imagined! I did not realize that being a full-time blogger was such a tough job. I loved blogging, but doing it for a paycheck was totally new to me. There was a part of me that thought being a blogger would be much easier than my jobs as a nonprofit professional or a fundraising executive…was I ever wrong.

The surprises continued. I did not realize that it would take so much effort to maintain a steady income. Being selected for paid opportunities did not happen as fast as I thought it would, and there was a big learning curve to accomplish what my coaches did on a daily basis. I learned the hard way that, while full-time blogging gives you an extraordinary amount of freedom and is amazing and fun, if you are not earning enough income, it can become a grind just like any other job.

Because I was caught off-guard, I ended up in a financial bind. Because I had to take on unavoidable debt, I was forced to go back to consulting. Blogging was not paying me enough to provide resources for my family. I was so taken by my initial success that I did not know what I did not know!

The demand for the Motivated Mom initiative was overwhelming. It took a while for me to swallow my pride, but I eventually had a real conversation with a friend, Dorinda Walker, a vice president of a Fortune 100 company and a thought leader, speaker, and financial guru in her own right. She was someone I trusted to give me the type of advice that superseded our friendship and would be based on the tenets of solid financial wellness. Dorinda was my original counsel who encouraged me to start the Motivated Mom initiative in the first place, and she was an avid supporter from the beginning. She was well aware of my humble beginnings, growth, challenges, and potential. And most of all, I knew that she would tell me the truth. Period.

I remember what she said to me like it was yesterday. "You need to get your butt back to work (your basic nine-to-five job) or get yourself some high-level clients." She used much more colorful language, but you get the idea. We laughed together for a few seconds, and as those words hit me, my reality set in. I knew instantly that she was right. I needed to rethink my business model; I could no longer let down my family or carry unnecessary debt.

Looking back, I now realize the leap to become a full-time blogger was very different from the leap I took to launch the Motivated Mom Tour. Hosting the Motivated Mom Tour came out of a place of love, passion, and a desire to help attendees become great women and extraordinary moms, with the hope that they raise their children with love and patience. With the tour, I only ever thought about planning events to empower moms. I was completely fine with hosting the tour, working with my clients, and running my consulting firm. I did not think that it would morph into a full-blown social media platform. In fact, that was the furthest thing from my mind.

But the leap to become a full-time blogger was another story entirely. I had to let go of everything familiar and take a risk. Now I know that I was not ready to leap when I did. At the time, I was not prepared, and it cost me dearly. It took almost two years for me to get out of debt and learn the ropes to become a true, professional blogger.

While I was committed to doing what I needed to grow my blog content, subscriptions, and social media presence to be an attractive competitor in the blog space, I was not schooled enough to do it properly.

I remember the first time I was denied an opportunity because I did not have enough followers. I was shocked! While I did not have a lot of followers, I certainly had a social media presence through my tour. That's when I realized that I had a lot of work left to do. And it was work that I had no idea *how to do*.

Even so, I worked hard to grow my social presence and expand my reach. Every evening I spent time liking and commenting on Instagram photos, sharing and commenting on other blog posts, and scheduling tweets for days at a time. I tried hiring companies that manage social media to grow my presence and expand my reach, but the problem was, I had no idea what I needed from them. So, I began using what I knew…my Motivated Moms Tour. I created a hashtag and promoted it in every city. I asked attendees to follow me on social media. And it worked! The saying is true…ask and you shall receive.

In addition to using my tour, I also followed the consistent advice of other bloggers that seemed to be a common thread in all of the articles I read about growing the number of my followers.

- I promoted my #MotivatedMom hashtag on all platforms and posts

- I used other funny, creative, and trending hashtags in my posts

- I commented on popular conversations and trending hashtags

- I followed and interacted with other bloggers

The Motivated Mom Tours were designed to give moms a space to network, learn, and share stories so that they could become better, more engaged parents. Little did I know that it would become the springboard to so much more. I knew that the tours were evolving into something amazing, but I did not know the amount of time that it would take for me to manage the new platform. I was completely prepared to continue on my path of working and doing the tours on the side.

But here is what happened…the tours evolved and birthed
the blog; the blog evolved and birthed a community; the
community evolved and birthed specialty events; and finally,
the specialty events evolved and birthed additional programs,
developed especially for moms. When I began to grow the
number of blog followers, my initial thought was, *Will I ever
get to five thousand?* While today I have an average of seventy
thousand viewers a month, it is an ongoing effort to gain
followers and honestly, I still view it as a challenge. In the
end, the blog has become an important part of my Motivated
Mom platform. And I now represent well-known Fortune 500
companies as a brand ambassador.

Each year I host a session to debrief and evaluate the previous
year and survey moms to determine their greatest needs and
keep the momentum going. In 2019, the Motivated Mom
platform launched several programs and initiatives to motivate,
empower, inspire, and equip moms to live a life of purpose,
in abundance and financially free, while practicing guilt-free
self-care.

Although I have only been blogging and managing the
Motivated Mom platform for a few years, I freely consult with
other bloggers, entrepreneurs, and aspiring entrepreneurs
on how they can grow their platform, raise money for their
initiative, or become a blogger. I offer them the same advice

that I received when I first began. I refer them to Elayna Fernandez to take the passion test. I recommend that they check out the content developed by Cameka Smith, founder of the BOSS Network, who shares strategies on becoming an entrepreneur and growing businesses on her site. I suggest specific bloggers to follow and blog posts to read to help build their social platforms. I am willing to pay it forward to encourage new enthusiasts, but I am not a *coach* per se, and I have no desire to be. But I will share what I know, and the rest is up to you.

> *"Most goals people set are not achieved because they are not held accountable for them. When goals are made in private, they tend to fall off because people stop being motivated, stop focusing and stop prioritizing."*
>
> —Bola Onada Sokunbi, *Goal Setting to Live Your Dreams*

There is much to be said about ensuring that you are held accountable while pursuing your purpose. Choosing several individuals who will continuously keep you sharp mentally, spiritually, and professionally will support and safeguard your success. It is practically a non-negotiable aspect of leaping. Let's be honest…who doesn't need a little help now and then?

Of course, there is a degree of vulnerability that comes with accountability, because it means that you are willing to reveal and stay true to your most authentic self. As you take your quantum leap toward your next level, having a faithful few to ground you will prove to be a vital part of your process. To be perfectly frank, there is no limit to the number of accountability checks and balances that you can have in place. Each one will help you move further along in your process.

However, there are two specific areas of answerability that I suggest you pay special attention to when leaping.

Moral accountability will rest on the shoulders of those who know and understand you at your core. Chances are, these individuals were present during your hatching process. They understand the trials and tribulations of your journey to this point.

As you leap into a new level, unscrupulous individuals may offer you shortcuts to success by any means possible. When you are deeply involved in working toward something so important, you may be wearing rose-colored glasses that make you an easy target. It is essential to have friends, colleagues, coaches, or mentors who can act as your voice of reason. They will help to ensure that you do not lose your way, no matter how tempting some of the more unsavory offers that come your way may seem.

Vision accountability is all about having an anchor for the vision that you plan to make into a reality. As you leap into a world of new possibilities, it can be easy to veer off the path of your original vision. It does not take much to wander off the mark.

I remember that, shortly after launching the Motivated Mom initiative, there were a few other opportunities that came my way. Several other entrepreneurs who did not know my true focus suggested that I follow the crowd and take advantage of these popular options. I thought heavily about it and decided not to follow through on their ideas. While these opportunities might have been profitable, they did not fit the path that I had envisioned for the Motivated Mom. I had a desire to serve the everyday working mom, and in some instances, the underserved. It took a friend to counsel me on ways to make the platform profitable, but it certainly did not mean altering my initial vision.

Keep this lesson in mind when weighing the opportunities that come your way. It is helpful to have trusted advisors on your side to ensure you remain vision-aligned. They will help you with suggestions that guarantee you will not compromise your vision to achieve success.

I am blessed to have a few people in my life to hold me accountable. My husband Andre remains at the top of the list as the most important influencer for my decisions. He is my sounding board, my biggest cheerleader, and the first to tell me to pursue my dreams. He is also the first to tell me when I should pause. I believe I am a great reader of people, but I happen to give most the benefit of the doubt…way too often! Thankfully, Andre has a keener eye than me when it comes to this talent. He has often shared his thoughts about people we meet. In the past, when I went with my gut and did not listen to his sage advice, I paid dearly. I have come to use him as my guiding light.

Having my husband as my primary accountability partner is essential. Not only do we look out for each other, we have been given the humbling opportunity to parent an amazing little boy, our son Chance. When anything comes between us on our ability to care for Chance, we take immediate action to rectify the situation. knowing that if it is in his best interest, it is in our best interest as well.

I realize that you may not be married or have children, and that's more than okay. But please find an accountability partner…not just for your business, but for life's big decisions.

We all need to be surrounded by people who are truthful, smart, and loving to help keep us level and grounded. A hype man may be good for a party where you have a good time, but when it is time to get back to real life, you do not want or need the hype; you want to succeed!

Here are a few ideas to work on regarding your leap.

- Identify three potential accountability partners and three potential counselors.

- Determine what you need to learn before you can leap to your next level.

- Transform your life by nullifying procrastination.

Once of the greatest assets that you can acquire on the journey toward fulfillment, success, and happiness is new knowledge. That knowledge can come because you have taken a class, or because you have reached out to a person in the position to mentor you; either way, I know that it will prove to be rich and incredibly valuable. As I built up the belief that I could attempt something new and work to develop the potential inside of me, I was so thankful to find others who had gone before me and paved the way. I gained so much insight about what to do and what NOT to do, simply by asking and being willing to be taught. No matter how much you grow, always remaining in the position of a learner is a definite way to ensure that you continue to position yourself to succeed!

Chapter Six

Propel

"The value of a moment is immeasurable. The power of just ONE moment can propel you to success and happiness or chain you to failure and misery."

—Steve Maraboli

With all my heart, I believe in the following quote by Steve Maraboli, best-selling author, behavioral scientist, and sought-after speaker: "The value of a moment is immeasurable. The power of just one moment can propel you to success and happiness or chain you to failure and misery." I can attest that things can change in a moment. In the blink of an eye, you can find yourself on another level in your business, in a better financial situation, or happier than you've ever been. In the same manner, you can experience a level of failure that is so epic you wonder how you will ever recover or bounce back. I have experienced both.

I have propelled in what seemed to be an instant, and I have also failed in ways that made me feel like my life had no meaning. For example, sometimes it seemed as if the Motivated Mom platform grew by leaps and bounds overnight. I was doing so well that it was difficult to keep up with the demand. Then again, when I planned and activated the first Motivated Mom Retreat, I took such a loss financially that I thought I would never get out of debt.

If you feel you need new possibilities to appear in your life, then it is important to create a goal—not a highly ambitious one, but instead one that will bring you passion, joy, and the fulfillment of being involved. Initially setting achievable goals will likely propel you to setting even loftier goals that inspire you to move upward and far above your present reach. Visualize your dreams and goals, great and small. Keeping the vision in your head will definitely motivate you to stay on track and pursue your desired success. Be joyfully and absolutely involved in whatever your next "moment" is.

Almost everyone has had the chance to see a bird glide through the sky effortlessly. Did that bird go to flight school, take a certification test, obtain a license? Not a chance. For a bird, the act of flying is intuitive and instinctive. For humans, the flying takes precise science, skill development, and a network of people working together to support human flight. So much calculated effort goes into ensuring that an aircraft's propellers are in full rotation and ready to take off. Likewise, when you are ready to fly, you too must be equipped to propel. Being fully equipped to propel is all about having the right individuals with you to ignite, build, and sustain the momentum that is necessary for soaring.

Having a team of people around you who believe in your vision and mission is critical to propel into flight and sustain that flight after takeoff. You may need people who are smarter than you, specialists in key areas and skilled laborers who can help you to launch. They too must want you to succeed and be personally vested in your success. It is not to your advantage to have yes-men around you who will not give critical advice based on analytical thinking. You need people who will honestly tell you the negative forecast and stand by to help you navigate through it if necessary.

It is especially important to have individuals around who can carry out what you are not yet up to speed on completing. These individuals know their lane and are committed to excelling in it in on behalf of your takeoff.

Think of the air traffic controller and the airplane mechanic, who have completely different roles, but their concerted efforts and expertise are both vital to ensuring a flight will take off. You need to ensure that you have people in place who are qualified and consummate in their efforts in adding an extra measure of faith to your leap. The two types of people that you should try to attract to help you are those who have *position* and those who have *passion*. It is completely up to you to understand the difference.

There are several definitions for the word *position*. The most common interpretations are "the act of placing or arranging" and "official rank or status." These descriptions are important to you because those who have position will you see your potential and possibility, although they may not believe in you or have passion regarding your individual success. Many times, their support of you is actually to use your platform to better position themselves in the future. With this wisdom, proceed accordingly—not with a jaded eye or a negative approach, but with an open, honest, and informed assessment. Sometimes it may be difficult to distinguish their motives, but time will always tell.

I have experienced countless situations with people in certain positions who had the power to help yet tried to take advantage of my trust in any way they could. I remember working as a consultant for an NFL player to manage all of his foundation's fundraising efforts. I jumped in headfirst and created several campaigns and events that could be implemented throughout the year. I designed and executed programs, engaged the community, and created press opportunities for the overall mission of the foundation (contacting the press was not in my contract, but it was in my heart to go the extra mile).

I was working directly with the NFL player and his family, and not too long into this gig, I realized that I was in a very unique situation. Why? Because I had not yet met the executive managing director of the foundation. I was introduced to him via email and, eventually, we talked on the phone a few times, but he was not extremely involved with the activities that I was responsible for planning.

I did think it was a little weird, since he was a nonprofit professional and should have been overseeing my activities. Along the way, I found out that he was managing the foundation through a talent agency, so he was not a direct employee. At this point, I had a better understanding of his role and the situation began to make more sense. After nearly two years of working on campaigns for the foundation and planning its second large fundraiser, I finally met the executive managing director.

He made an appearance approximately three weeks before the big event. He was full of compliments about all of the "amazing" work I had accomplished and how he wanted me on his team to work with other celebrity foundations. He also told me how experienced I was and that I would be a great partner for him.

After two years, I thought that his appearance on the scene was definitely odd. But because I was so deeply involved, and I was in the final three weeks of planning this huge event, I ignored the "red flags" flying right in front of me. I should have paid more attention to my initial feeling that something was off.

You have probably guessed what happened next. To my surprise, just three days after our meeting, the executive managing director started barking orders at me and telling me what *we* were going to do. He demanded that I give him all of my sponsorship contacts and include him on my sponsorship activation calls. He also made a big stink about my process with my client to try to cause friction between us and to get his way. This diversion nearly worked.

He was very keen for me to bring him up to speed on my activation plans. While I did send him my sponsorship reports, I did *not* include my contacts. Wouldn't you know, one week before the event, he scheduled a call with my client to present *my* work as his own. But, because I had worked with my client's family more than with him directly, the imposter took for granted that I was not in communication with the client. Now, he was in for a surprise.

He scheduled a meeting with my client and the talent agency executives to present my work and claimed all of the credit for the fundraising, with exception of five thousand dollars. He strongly suggested that they fire me and let him manage the big event. Luckily for me, my client's family told me everything that happened. Initially, I was disappointed, and then I become extremely angry. The family asked me what I'd like to see happen with the executive managing director, and I told them to move forward with the event. I suggested that they hold off on talking to him about his actions until afterwards. The event was just a few weeks away, and emotions were running high.

In the end, I hosted one of the best fundraisers ever for my client. It was named one of the top events of the NBA All-Star Weekend, and I was given full credit for my work. The executive director attended and watched. I do not know what my client or the talent agency said to him, but I do know that I continue to do work for my client without him being a factor.

I did not know this initially (and sometimes neither will you), but I soon learned that he was in it for the glory. He wanted to use my talents to position himself to appear effective to the client and the agency. He was buttering me up only to throw me under the bus and take credit for my work for his personal gain.

On the other hand, there will be certain individuals in your world who have an undeniable passion to see you succeed. Passion happens to be my word of the year 2019. It is defined as an "intense, driving or overmastering feeling of conviction."

These passionate individuals will want to help you in any way possible, even if their skills, contributions, or connective abilities are minimal. Harness their energy and position them to grow with you as you begin your way up and away.

Learning how and where to lean is paramount as you get ready to leap into flight. Leaning is like standing over a cliff with a roaring river below. You want to glance over the edge to experience the beauty of the river, but you cannot put all of your weight forward, or you will tilt over and become engulfed by the canyon below. It is dangerous to lean too heavily on those who have position because, the more you lean, the more indebted to them you will become.

I'm not sure if this has ever happened to you, but it has happened to me several times; individuals agree to help you and then, once you accomplish great things, they claim your success as their doing. They want you to treat them, pay them, and acknowledge them as if your contribution and your dream were not as significant as their role in making it happen for you. I know that sometimes people can be so self-absorbed that they believe their talents, abilities, and connections are more beneficial than they are in reality.

My advice is the same when it comes to leaning too heavily on those who have passion but come up a little short on skills. You may overload them with your vision and not get the quality help you need to move forward. I have trusted several passionate people, and I know too well how this turns out. They are eager to help you move your vision forward, but they lack the necessary knowledge to do so. But because they are willing, you give them a shot. There have been times where I trusted passionate people in my life with big tasks, and I was not happy with the results. I lost time and money and ultimately had to have the task done over again the right way.

What I learned through both experiences is that learning is a balancing act.

- You can go left, right, forward, or back and still maintain your footing. The more you lean, the more you learn balance.

- When it comes to assessing those in position and those with passion, make sure you know who you are dealing with to position yourself to sustain flight.

- Do not be afraid, ashamed, or too shy to ask for what you need to help you achieve success.

The one final piece to put in place as you prepare to leap is your family. As you strategically build your support team, be sure to do so with your family's agreement and full support. Since family members are usually the first and last impacted by the commitments, sacrifices, highs, and lows of your venture, find out if and how they are vested in your journey. Be clear on how much support you will be asking from them and what you envision *before* you leap. It is best to sit down with your family to discuss candidly what your venture will cost, as well as what will be gained. There are many ways that costs can be incurred when leaping, monetary but also time, energy, and focus. Your family members have a right to know how these costs may directly impact them.

I remember sitting on the sofa, watching television, while responding to work emails. My son was playing with his toy cars and talking to me at the same time. He walked up to the edge of the sofa and started asking me a bunch of questions. I was responding while still engrossed in responding to emails. His fight for my attention went on for a few minutes. Finally, he said, "Mommy, talk to me with your eyes." I was stunned. I looked up at him with tears in my eyes and said, "Sure baby, Mommy is so sorry. What do you want to talk to me about?" That conversation forever changed me as a mom. I realized that I had to be present for my son when he needed me.

One of the most expensive *costs* that you will incur in leaping is the magnitude of time you spend on it, often taking away from day-to-day family time. While there are so many exciting outcomes that will come from leaping into your purposed place, it is going to require a substantial amount of time. Invariably, the time you spend will either take away from or dilute the time spent with others. It is so important to count this cost up front. Setting clear expectations, boundaries, and communication methods with your family will help preserve a safe haven for the importance of the family unit.

"The reason many people fail is not for lack of vision but for lack of resolve and resolve is born out of counting the cost."

—Robert H. Goddard

When I took the leap out of fundraising and discontinued working with my clients in that sector, my family and I suffered financially. I felt like I needed to break with my clients so that I could focus on what I needed to do for myself. In my new line of business, developing the Motivated Mom charter, it could take weeks, months, or sometimes years to get a yes for sponsorships, contracts, or influencer opportunities. The Motivated Mom business was gaining recognition at such a fast pace, I decided I needed to direct all of my attention to it.

As I moved into establishing the tour, I realized that it would take much more than the initial sponsorship investment I received from a Fortune 500 company to move my vision forward. But I did not know how much more until my husband and I had to dig into our own savings, a little more than thirty thousand dollars, to ensure the Motivated Mom Tour was going to happen. It was time for me to rethink my leap—and quickly. Believe me, my husband agreed with that call.

One of my nicknames for Andre is the walking calculator, so he was already six steps ahead of me in his thought process. He knew what I did not—that we could not use our precious savings to fund my business, and that I'd have to figure out another way. We sat down and developed a budget we both could live with. Over the next few years, I worked to triple what I had raised for the first tour, to make it happen from a solid business standpoint.

Perhaps you are a single mother who has hatched and stands on the cliff of change. Your contemplation of leaping into a new level of life may be slightly different, because your support system may rest a little more heavily on external means. Nonetheless, the potential for your success and impact are still great. Still, consider what is needed in order for you to move forward, and who is available to be the network of support for you as you leap forward. Surround yourself with those who have proven able to be innovative in accomplishing tasks and glean from their wisdom. It is worth the effort to connect with individuals who are willing and able to support your leap and who will alleviate your sacrifice.

There is so much value in investing the energy and effort to ensure that you have the right team and momentum before you leap. It may take a few rounds of having collaborative conversations, putting the pieces in place, and assessing them for effectiveness. If you have the willingness to make the necessary adjustments, in the end, it will all have been worth your trouble.

Just as the propellers on the helicopter or plane take a moment to get cranked up and ready for flight, so it is with making sure that you have built the best base and support team.

- Learn how to decipher if a person has position, passion or both.

- Ensure that you have the right team members.

- Share the costs of time, effort, and money with your family before you leap.

Leaping = Real Success

What a powerful example of success. Yes, leaping is real success. To leap is to go after something that you want or something that you were created to do, always believing that you will eventually fly.

> *"We must walk consciously only part way toward our goal, and then leap in the dark to our success."*
>
> —Henry David Thoreau

Leaping is a powerful force, propelling you from a place of comfort to an accomplished goal. Give yourself permission to stand on the edge of *What if?* and leap into *What is next?*

What situation or event in your life is making you feel you are being called to leap?

_____

_____

_____

_____

What's holding you back from taking a leap?

What makes you doubt yourself? Where did that self-doubt begin?

What are a few actions you can take to boost your confidence to make the leap?

How have courage, proper positioning, and propelling helped you on your path to success?

Section Three

Soar

Chapter Seven

Wing Span

"I have a six foot eight wingspan on a five foot eleven body—I can dunk. My wingspan allows me to do a lot of things that other people at my height might not be able to do."

—Odell Beckham, Jr.

Y ou may have heard of the athletic ability of the New York Giants' Odell Beckham Jr. on the professional football field. However, when you hear that he has a more than six-and-a-half-foot wingspan, you might calculate that he is a large guy with a great reach. What is more interesting is that he knows his own capacity and what he can accomplish with that expansive reach. The same is true for you. As you leap into new levels and progressively pursue the best version of yourself, be clear about exactly how far your *wingspan* reaches.

The physical property of wingspan is determined by the distance from the tip of one wing or arm to the tip of the other. This measurement does not seem that relevant on the surface, but when you consider the heights that a bird, plane, or human desires to reach, wingspan takes on more importance. Plainly put, the more wingspan you possess, the more territory you can cover...literally.

As you prepare to soar in your endeavors, become more keenly aware of what is essential to reach your potential. Honestly assess what is within reach and what is not in your sphere of influence, at least for the time being. Then make your decisions based on your wingspan.

I often look to the simple but profound directions found in the Serenity Prayer that say, "God grant me the serenity to accept the things I cannot change, the courage to change the things I can, and the wisdom to know the difference." As you prepare to soar, make sure that your success can be sustained. I encourage you to learn your wingspan and to fly high accordingly!

In 2016, I found myself once again at the beginning of a new year and waiting intently for the universe to share my next word with me. As surely as it took the time to become aware of my next venture, my direction came through with the word *soar.* I was excited about the possibilities of what the new year was about to bring. My hatching and leaping had proved to be completely transformative. At this point, each step in the process had meaning and was instrumental in bringing me closer to my purpose of reaching and motivating women in ways that I had not previously imagined.

During that season, I came to know the true power of self-discovery and how it is connected to living a fulfilled life. I learned that it is quite okay to ask myself questions such as, *What do I really enjoy doing? What would I do for free for sheer pleasure if money was not a factor?* Hatching was about answering those tough questions with true answers! Leaping was equally meaningful, because it was then that I mustered up the courage and confidence to leave my comfort zone in order to pursue my purpose. There were many lessons and inner changes along the way, all of which were a part of the greater plan. I could tell that it was time for me to soar.

When I think of the image of the word *soar,* what comes
to mind is an eagle gliding through the sky. And there is
something about the way an eagle flies that looks different than
every other ordinary bird. An eagle's flight appears to be more
confident and deliberate. Even if an eagle's initial exit from the
nest is shaky, by the time human eyes see it in flight, the bird's
wingspan is something to behold. An eagle definitely soars
through the sky with purpose.

By definition, *wingspan* means, "The maximum extent across
the wings of an aircraft or of a bird or other flying animal,
measured from tip to tip and by design." A bird's wingspan
is created symmetrically balanced, and, as long as it is not
overloaded or unbalanced, it can continue to soar.

This makes the bird an essentialist. It only carries things
that are necessary. This makes perfect sense for the bird that
does not have any cargo or concerns. Perhaps it is not quite
as simple for you and me, who by life's design, collect quite a
number of things and people throughout our lives. As you seek
to spread your wings and rise in purpose, how do you make
sure that your wingspan remains balanced? How do you ensure
that you are an essentialist and only carry what you need?

Well, becoming an essentialist means that you have to learn
how to separate, discard, and relinquish the people and things

that have been a part of your former existence but do not have a place in your next season.

If you are true to yourself, you will find that many of your present relationships are not bad, but they are not essential. You also may begin to realize that some of the activities you are involved in may be profitable but not purposeful, and therefore are not essential. So, what happens to your relationships that may no longer be essential?

You learn to set boundaries.

Understand that it takes a lot of courage to set boundaries. For years, I had heard others talk about setting these lines of demarcation, but quite honestly, I had never really implemented them in my life. I used to think that I did not have a need for them, that my life was completely balanced.

But then, I recall a conversation with my blog coach Elayna one day, when she candidly pointed out my lack of boundaries and offered a few examples of how they were affecting my purpose. All of a sudden, it hit me like a ton of bricks. My eyes turned as big as saucers. I would not even let her finish her thought before I burst out and said, "Oh my goodness. That's what God has been saying to me during my quiet time. I need to set boundaries." A huge smile came across Elayna's face as she continued to share with me how setting boundaries would make things clearer for me.

Before my epiphany, all I had thought about was the top-charting song recorded by Mary J. Blige, "Love No Limits." Take a look at the lyrics when you have a moment. My attitude came through whenever I heard that song. Who needed boundaries? I wanted to help everyone I loved. It's not that there is anything wrong with doing for others. In fact, with the many roles you may play in the course of a day, I would expect that you are going to give much to the ones you love. However, problems arise when the needs of others supersede your own. And even when you know that you should stop and prioritize your self-care, there is a good chance you will persist...unless you set up the necessary boundaries!

I was always willing to give my all to anyone who needed help, and I often sacrificed the time I needed for myself. I would deflect and focus on others' needs instead of dealing with my own. I think it was partially due to my unwillingness to deal with my low self-worth; it seemed easier to help others. It was not until I noticed how regularly I was dealing with health issues and depression that I vowed to take better care of myself and keep some of the energy I was giving out freely.

Boundaries sounded so restrictive to me before, but now I get it. Setting boundaries is like being free. Living free does not mean I do what I want; it means that I am free to live my life the way I was purposed to without feeling guilty or bound to others. Boundaries give me permission and freedom to focus on what I was created to do in this life and to eliminate any and all things that were a hindrance to being able to do them at an optimal level.

Once you too begin to understand the truth, be ready to fearlessly set boundaries so that you can live a life of purpose and abundance—mentally, emotionally, spiritually, and even financially free. In order to set proper boundaries that will actually allow you to soar, there are a few things you need to do first. Follow my lead and reflect on what I have done to complete my journey. It helps to continually evaluate your personal and professional life and set up a plan of action which includes the following:

- *Search yourself.* Get to know yourself. Become familiar and comfortable with what is important to you, including your feelings, beliefs, emotions, and ideas.

- *Detach yourself.* Provide yourself with the space needed to separate your thoughts, feelings, and goals from those of your peers to gain a healthy perspective without creating conflict within yourself.

- *Respect yourself.* Always tell yourself that you are more than the sum of your mistakes. Fully respect yourself and give others in your life the permission to do the same.

- *Decide for yourself.* You own the right to make a decision or change your mind. You only owe people what you are willing to give.

By setting boundaries, you will allow yourself to take care of your own needs by saying no to requests and people that do not serve your purpose. You will then have more freedom to focus on what is important to you. For me, it was my health, family, and future. Here is my short list:

- Protect my physical and emotional space from distractions that can potentially steer me off track.

- Become more creative in my writing, speaking, and extracurricular activities.

- Teach people how to treat me with respect and care.

Do you see the need for boundaries in your own life? Where can you cut back, and where can you add freedom? Are you willing to explore those places and, slowly but surely, begin implementing boundaries where they are needed?

I know now that having boundaries in life is critically important. Not only will it free you from the frustration you feel when you do not take care of yourself, but it will teach people how to treat you. This is critically important, and I personally believe that we share a great deal of responsibility for the way others treat us. Perhaps you are presently like I used to be, and you think that you can passively teach others how to treat you by not addressing their unacceptable behavior. I am here to tell you that passivity does not really work.

My good friend Yvonne McNair, founder of the events and entertainment marketing company, Captivate Marketing Group, teaches people how to treat her by calling them out with composure and kindness. She often claims, "When you turn your passion into a business, you learn to take the emotion out of it."

An Emmy-nominated event producer, Yvonne has a wealth of brand management expertise with entertainment, corporate, and nonprofit clients. Her career includes creating innovative marketing campaigns and event management for top brands and numerous media and entertainment companies such as Sundance Film Festival, VH1, NBC, and MTV.

Yvonne spent many years working with the late, great Prince and his protégé, Liv Warfield. Yvonne was also responsible for Prince's record-breaking performance at the Essence Festival in 2014, along with turning the Superdome purple to commemorate the thirtieth anniversary of *Purple Rain*.

With all her accomplishments, she still had to learn that, when she worked with her clients, she had to keep balance in her life. In an *Essence* article, Yvonne shared a pivotal learning moment in her career and how the lesson propelled her forward.

Yvonne said:

> I want to start with some great advice that I got from Doug E. Fresh. One day he said that his approach is that, "I am good with you winning as long as I am not losing." That one pearl of wisdom resonated with me on so many levels. The advice changed my approach on how I work with clients and it was one of those life lessons in which I learned to always maintain a balance with my priorities. We can all win together but I will never put myself in a situation where I am going to lose by working with someone.

Understand that teaching people how to treat you may cause you a bit of initial discomfort. But you will find, as I did, that temporary uneasiness is far better than dealing with the resentment you will feel building inside of you if you did not respect yourself enough to demand to be treated fairly.

I was empowered when I embraced the fact that it is never too late to change how you feel about yourself. I could not complain about how I was being treated when I taught people close to me how to treat me. A good friend once told me, "Whatever treatment you have accepted in the past will be repeated in the future." For too long I had placed the needs of others above my own, and they took whatever energies I was happy to give them. I had to learn and agree to be honest about when I could, and when I could not, give of myself anymore.

Before learning to set healthy boundaries, I would agree to help even when I did not want to. I would say yes to projects because I did not want to be seen as selfish. I would commit myself to tasks that would not offer a mutual benefit, and that sometimes would end up as an expense to me. I realize now that I was only hurting myself. Being selfish is not a bad thing, especially when you can use a little love of self. We are to love our neighbors as ourselves; that means we are to love ourselves first.

Perhaps you have struggled with setting boundaries. Or you may have set boundaries but not stuck to your guns with implementing them. Now is the time! If you are going to live your life with purpose and on purpose, then setting boundaries is absolutely essential. What do you need to do to ensure that you stick to the boundaries that you've set? Let's become a better version of ourselves together!

Holding onto relationships, roles, or responsibilities that may seem harmless, but are not essential, can prove to be the difference between rising and sinking. I can remember doing some serious shedding during this season of my life. I was right on the brink of my new horizon, and, in order to rise to the full potential of the moment, I had to have some very honest conversations with myself and with my family. We had to take a close look at the lifestyle that we were currently living and what would have to be adjusted in order for us to collectively get to the next level. I knew that my sacrifice would ultimately be a sacrifice on their behalf as well.

That process ended with me deciding to release several clients. Just think about what that meant to me. Those clients were the result of hours spent cultivating relationships, but even more than that, they were sources of income. However, I instinctively knew that they would inevitably take away from my new purpose. I need to invest my time, effort, and energy into my new initiatives. And I knew that I could not soar with so many other contracts and business obligations.

I had to trust my desire to take flight, let go of clients to pick up partners, and take only what was essential to soar. There will always be numerous things that you have to eliminate as you begin to soar to new heights. Some of these things may include people who do not believe, negative thoughts, and memories of the past that are not beneficial. If you are anything like me, they will have to be routinely removed again and again, as they will invariably begin to creep back into your life if you allow them.

In addition, it is also best to banish any self-defeating thoughts and comparisons of yourself to others. Thoughts, things, and people must be routinely scrutinized, and only those that are absolutely imperative and essential for flight can be carried on your wings to deliver you to your next purposed place.

Soaring is flying high above anything you ever imagined. It is being yourself. It is living life on purpose.

Soaring means being intentional about everything you do. Trials you may experience are the preparation required to build a thick skin, like armor, to face the next internal or external battle you will have to face when you are walking in your purpose. There will always be battles to fight, but you will be prepared, like me, to take Dorinda's advice: "Do not sit still and cry, asking, 'Why me?' You will face each encounter head-on and say, 'Try me. Because there is nothing you can do to stop me.' "

You will have days when it feels as if the whole world is against you. There will be times when things are not going right, and the good stuff seems too far away. This is when you need to dig deep, use all the things you've learned to calm yourself, and do not panic! Do not let the setbacks set you back. Keep your thoughts positive, and use your hands and mind to work on your plan.

The wingspan is all about your bandwidth and your ability to hold and carry. Ultimately, you cannot allow yourself to get overloaded with so much that you cannot expand yourself. You have to be able to fully spread your wings in order to soar.

- Identify the boundaries you need to set.

- Start teaching people how to treat you.

- Identify what you can leave idle for a while you focus on your purpose.

Chapter Eight

Achieve Balance

"I believe that being successful means having a balance of success stories across the many areas of your life. You cannot truly be considered successful in your business life if your home life is in shambles."

—Zig Ziglar

I t is an amazing feeling to watch the fruits of your labor blossom and to experience the sense of happiness that comes from knowing you have accomplished your goals. It is an equally horrible feeling to have that reality interrupted by a whirlwind of unfinished work or forgotten obligations that appear at just the wrong moment. That is why, as you hatch, leap, and soar into each level in your life, it is essential that you work to maintain balance in each area of your life.

There is no better illustration of the delicate art of balance than watching a tightrope walker skillfully and gingerly move from one point to another. The acrobat manages to methodically navigate the rope with great precision and calculated care.

In thinking about all that goes into achieving a life of total fulfillment, real success, and true happiness, there are a few lessons to glean from the balancing act that the tightrope walker demonstrates. She is clearly focused on the end point, which is a must for you as you expand your horizons. Suppose your end goal is a collective of each of the pieces of your life. With that in mind, while you begin hatching and leaping in one area of your life, you cannot lose sight of or totally neglect the other areas that surround you.

Think about an eagle: From the ground, it looks as if the eagle soars majestically. The only thing you can observe from your vantage point is the slight movement of the bird's head from right to left, which is to maintain balance. However, as the eagle soars, it also encounters extreme temperature changes, turbulence, and wind swirl. It has to shift and make many in-the-moment decisions. It is impossible to decipher the bird's attitude when it flies at such a high altitude. The same will be true for you; the higher you soar, the more obstacles you will encounter.

After hosting the Motivated Mom Tour for two years, I made a decision to hold off on the tour and offer a Motivated Mom Retreat. I had been dealing with a few health issues and needed to focus on self-care. I knew that moms who were following me also lacked the ability to be intentional about self-care. The retreat was my way to offer motivation, inspiration, education, and guilt-free self-care experiences for moms.

During the first night of the retreat, I was in bed and should have been fast asleep. But at three in the morning, I began tossing and turning quite a bit; I could not relax. I turned on my back because my left arm started going numb, which I thought was due to me laying on it. Some time later, I felt a lot of pain in my left shoulder and my arm started tingling, so I sat straight up in the bed. I began shaking my arm, trying to ease the numbness, but it was not working. That's when I realized something was very wrong. I grabbed my blood pressure wrist monitor to find my blood pressure at an extremely high 197/154. I was at risk of having a stroke.

I was terrified and needed immediate help. My doctor's office was closed, so I phoned a nurse. Once I told her how high my blood pressure was, she found the nearest urgent care center for me. After spending a few hours there, I was released and able to get back to my retreat. I was told to take it easy and get plenty of rest. As hard as it was for me to miss a lot of the retreat, I listened to the experts and took care of myself. I hung back and watched a few activities, then made my way back to my room to rest.

I was upset that I was missing so much, but I knew that I had an amazing team in place which was more than capable of keeping things going. Then I began thinking about what the attendees would think of me for not being present for much of the event. I eventually found out that no one even knew that I was ill. Because I popped in and out of activities, no one even realized how much I was missing. Honestly, they were too busy enjoying all the activities I had planned for them. That was a huge lesson for me and confirming as well. As I began to soar, I found the need for balance.

> *"When you find peace within yourself, you will become the kind of person who can live at peace with others."*

—Peace Pilgrim (born Mildred Lisette Norman)

I usually spend my days rushing. If not running around physically, my mind is usually churning with a litany of thoughts: *What do I need to do next? I should have done that by now! Oh no, I did that wrong. I could have done better.* I needed a detour from my thoughts. I took a deep breath, and for the first time in a long while, I silenced myself. In those moments of stillness, I realized how to celebrate my progress and find balance. I learned how to find peace in the moment.

How do you handle all that may come with higher heights? Will you become flustered or remain focused? Do you deal with matters by exuding confidence, or do you project conceit? Often, people confuse confidence and conceit, as if they were similar, but they are not. Confidence is a feeling of self-assurance arising from appreciating your own abilities or qualities. It is simply being comfortable and feeling good about the skin that you inhabit. Conceit, on the other hand, means excessive pride in yourself. While conceited people seem self-confident on the outside, they are often insecure and unhappy with who they are.

"Confidence is a practice and a skill. It's not about being an extrovert and it's certainly not a personality trait. Everyone has the ability to be confident in any given situation with the right mindset and practice."

—Kim Stone, Undercover Mum

Australia-based Kim Stone, founder of Undercover Mum, coach and mentor, has said that confidence is a practice and a skill. I could not agree more. For most of my life, I have struggled with my confidence. The confidence lesson was not an easy one for me. However, I knew that if I was going to soar, I needed to learn to love myself with all my imperfections. Be forewarned, it certainly did not happen overnight. Regardless, confidence is the best gift you can give yourself. It will definitely play a vital role in your success.

What I have come to know is that, no matter what, it is vitally important to always remain humble and balanced when you are soaring. Do not forget that it is your own confidence and composure that ultimately causes you to soar and keeps you successfully in flight. And because that is true, you can always do what is required to reflect that belief in your behaviors. Even as you achieve new accomplishments and measures of your success are revealed, do not forget all of the personal shedding and growing that it took to get to this point.

This reminds me of a parable I once heard of a bird that had grown tired and found a tree branch to rest. While perched there, a strong storm rolled through and began blowing the branch violently, almost to the point of breaking. Even through the storm, the bird was not worried. Why? The bird was confident that if the branch broke, he would be able to fly with his own two wings. He saw that the tree had many other branches where he could rest. The bird accepted his own vulnerability and the benefits that the tree provided. The bird could have easily been a victim of a broken branch, but instead, he accepted the reality of what was before him and found a new truth.

No matter where you go, it is important to stay grounded. One of the quickest ways to make sure that you do just that is to not allow yourself to become intoxicated by the success of soaring. Constant compliments and flattery are just two of the things that can lead to intoxication and a loss of focus. Relationships with individuals who are unbalanced themselves, and even your own pride, also may also get in your way.

Staying grounded is easier said than done, especially with the "instant" fame that can come from social media. There was a time when I allowed the opinions of others to dictate my plans for the Motivated Mom platform. I was told that I needed to charge for coaching, build a program where people would pay me monthly, or charge moms to join a network…the list went on and on. For a month or two (okay, maybe a bit longer, but definitely not for an entire season of my life), I actually entertained these ideas. They were tough to resist. I was not making the amount of money that I wanted with the platform, and I was contributing all the funds I earned to increase the impact of my initiative.

This was the wrong way to keep my business going, and I knew it. I remembered what Cameka Smith once told me: "If your business isn't making money, then it's just a hobby." Cameka was trying to help me understand that I could not stay afloat with one foot in my personal funds and the other in my business funds.

So I challenged myself to name three things I had done to become financially secure in my business as an entrepreneur. This was an important task to complete, since I needed to turn things around quickly.

- *I created and used a budget.* A budget will help you keep track of income and expenses. It's important to know what's coming in and going out. This goes for your personal as well as business dealings.

- *I identified strategies for monetization.* Institute several streams of income and stay ahead of the curve. Do not wait until you need money to think about ways to earn it.

- *I treated my clients well.* Treating people well is the best way to attract and retain more clients. I may not always be the top performer, and that's okay, but I always treat my clients well so that they come back and share news about my talents with others.

These tips helped me to monetize my business, and, when I implemented them well, they worked again and again. However, I still struggled with direction and next steps concerning my overall strategy. After thinking things through, I sat down and wrote down my reasons *why*. You see, I had forgotten why I started Motivated Mom in the first place. I forgot that it was never about me or my ego; it was always about motivating and inspiring moms to be great women. My definition of "great" means whole, secure, happy, fulfilled, and healthy, so that the moms that followed me would raise their children better. My fulfillment and happiness were never tied to my own fame or station.

I needed strategies and willpower to help me accomplish a larger goal. Willpower is best achieved by having a great reason *why*. A great *why* is a meaningful connection to your goal. Your *why* is found by asking yourself, *Why am I doing this? What's the reason behind my desire to accomplish it?*

Therefore, if you begin to veer off your path of fulfillment, understanding your *why* will help you keep track of where you stand in your efforts. Be aware of your *why*, and it will serve as safety rails to gently nudge you back to the center of your inspiration. But beware, once you understand yourself and find a new place of clarity regarding your identity, it will not be long before that very identity in you is challenged.

> *"You can never leave footprints that last if you are always walking on tiptoe."*
>
> —Leymah Gbowee

It is to be expected that, when you begin to climb new heights, you will encounter all sorts of barriers. It has happened before, whenever you moved through hatching and leaping. Now it is time to work out the roadblocks of soaring.

Once you start soaring, you will look down (and, in some cases, up) to see all eyes on you. Some people will be smiling and cheering you on; others will be aiming weapons at you, hoping to bring you down, while still others will be calling for you to come back to a place and time that has nothing to do with your purposed future. This is when trusting yourself is critically important. Without trusting myself, I lived in fear and anxiety. I doubted myself, worried, competed, and tried to control every single outcome. It was exhausting. Trusting myself freed me from fear. Yes, initially it seemed ridiculous and foolish. That's until I changed the direction of my trust compass. I had been thinking too negatively, not believing that I would win. When I began trusting myself instead of the fear, I could see myself soaring.

Think of a time when you felt everything was going as planned. The kids were acting civilized, your boss was understanding your recommendations on improvement, and you were getting along with your significant other. You were on cloud nine. Everything was coming together like a well-oiled machine. All of sudden, a tiny fiber of doubt began to niggle in your brain. You started to question your identity and wonder how you got to where you are.

Once you identify who you were created to be and start walking in your purpose, some kind of adversary will appear, with the goal of disqualifying all that you've accomplished so far. The process of shedding and discarding the lies about yourself that occurred during your hatching will be tested. It is likely that this antagonist will manifest itself in your mind.

We all have that voice in our head, attempting to convince us that we are less than our identified purpose. But you can quell your internal voice much more easily than the voices of the people who come into your life. Sometimes the individuals around you will be able to detect your insecurities, fears, and other elements that you are balancing, as they vie for a front-and-center position in your mind. When this happens, be careful about exposing your insecurities and weaknesses to the wrong individuals. It is a balancing act to be as honest as you can with others, while at the same time being wise enough that they cannot take advantage of you or exploit you. But, by being honest with yourself and soaring with your newly earned strengths, you will be able to maintain. It is all about balance.

Years ago, I came across a quote that read, "Passion makes complacency uncomfortable." I began to live by this motto and committed myself to seek beyond my complacency. I was eager to find my true passion and prosper doing it! These are five steps I followed to find my passion, and you can too!

1. *Identify what you love to do so much that you would do it for free.* All my life, I knew that I wanted to help people to be great, but I never knew exactly how. Then I became a mom and started to take notice. I would ask myself questions. I knew I wanted to continue to do work I loved but also have the flexibility of being home with my son. It was not long after that that I began my

journey to connect my desire to help others with what I do for a living.

2. *Believe in yourself and in your dreams.* After several attempts at entrepreneurship, I took a leap of faith and started a multi-city tour to motivate moms to be great women and extraordinary moms. Do not allow your experience or lack thereof to deter you. Some told me it would take years to build my brand and monetization, yet it took me less than a year. Not only did I make my passion profitable, I am helping others to do the same. Believe that what you want to do is possible.

3. *Count the cost and consider the bottom line.* While launching a brand and tour at the same time allowed me my fair share of teachable moments, I have grown (sometimes despite myself) to empower brands, along with thousands of women. I now take opportunities and overcome the obstacles in my path.

4. *Listen. Learn. Labor.* Surround yourself with a smart team of believers. Only work with people who believe in your mission, who will listen to you, and who you can learn from. You cannot do everything on your own.

5. *Keep balanced.* Stay true to your reasons for becoming who you were purposed to be without sacrificing those you love…including yourself. I have learned that, to be comfortable, I must be my true authentic self.

Balance starts with the notion that you cannot please everyone. Ironically, trying to do so will result in not pleasing anyone.

It is important to prepare yourself for the great deal of pressure that comes from soaring into the spotlight. The higher you go, the more people will expect from you. Balance checks become critical at this point. It is so easy to get caught up in the hype of what others may say is the *popular* way of doing things. Do not allow others to cause you to struggle with what they consider the *right* way. Take a pause to ensure that you do what feels right for you. Avoid performing an act versus being your authentic self. You should feel a sense of peace when you make a decision. Feeling a sense of peace is like an atlas for me. It leads me to a safe space within myself that I can return to when I feel overwhelmed or uneasy.

> *"Breathe. Let go. And remind yourself that this very moment is the only one you know for sure."*
>
> —Oprah Winfrey

Keep evaluating where your own motives start to lead you, as well as the advice, chatter, and opinions of those around you.

Distance yourself from anything that can be used to discredit you or hinder you from soaring. Always remember that *you* are the person reflected in the mirror each morning. This is about checking yourself and keeping yourself 100 percent honest. You are the only one who has the power to tell yourself the truth. The good news is that, if you remain faithful to yourself, the balance will come.

> *"When you want to face the truth, just look at the mirror.*
> *The mirror never lies."*
>
> —Rashmi Goel

- List which steps you need to take to get you to being more confident

- Create an action plan if you begin to veer off your path.

- Height maintenance is all about you checking yourself.

Chapter Nine

Freedom

"Everything that is really great and inspiring is created by the individual who can labor in freedom."

—Albert Einstein

F or most of my life, I have lived in fear; I lacked the drive to be my authentic self. But recently, especially as I sat down to write this book, I took a good look inward and realized that I am funny, talented, and inspiring. I have begun to genuinely love myself. As I took this journey to the deepest depths of my heart and soul, I remembered so many things I had once loved to do. And freely. I was not worried about what others thought or how many likes it would get me on social media. I followed my passions, and they led me to freedom. I am not saying that the only way to have freedom is to do what you are passionate about. But whatever you choose to do should bring meaning and freedom to your life.

One of the hardest things for me to do is to say, "No!" To this day, I often struggle with that word and its meaning. But lately, I have found a great deal of freedom in the word *no*; saying no to joining the crowd if I don't believe in its cause, or to spending money that I cannot afford or to actions that do not align with my morals and beliefs.

On the other hand, I have felt the powerlessness of being told no. No from a friend when I was in need; no from a brand partner that has sponsored my initiatives for the past three years; no from my husband about ideas that I thought were perfect ways to grow my business. Being told no is an opportunity for me to evaluate my ask, to ensure that it is in alignment with my purpose, expected outcome, and overall happiness. In a way, hearing the word "no" provides me with an incentive to stop, learn, think, and regroup.

Watching an eagle soar effortlessly through the sky can sometimes become commonplace. In fact, when you see an eagle, you *expect* it to soar. Prior to this journey, I seldom considered the process that it takes for eagles to get to that place of soaring. Now, whenever I see an eagle gaining access to the open sky to soar, I am definitely reminded of my own path of hatching, leaping, and soaring!

I recall my first Motivated Moms Tour. While I was willing to leap to my next level, the journey provided me a few sobering lessons. I also think about my introduction into the world of blogging that was less about the blogging and more about learning a whole new set of skills I had never tried before. Each point on the journey was a new place of self-discovery and a segue into becoming the woman I am today; the woman that I knew I could be. The journey gave me the feeling of freedom to wake up every day loving my life and loving who I am. It has led me to a life where I feel completely comfortable with myself and what I am doing to make an impact, not just for me, but for my family and every person I encounter.

This freedom is such a paradigm shift. Instead of being trapped by the need for approval or affirmations from others, I learned to accept the core of who I am and to love each and every part of her. When you arrive at that place of self-acceptance and self-love, that is when you will soar on the heights over the earth.

You see, I am a firm believer that love transforms us. It connects us to ourselves, others, and our humanity. By unlocking the love flow to myself from myself, I came to the realization that love is not how I feel about myself, but rather how I treat myself. Loving myself was like working out. The more I work out, the more I develop and grow my muscles. My love for self was hidden behind years of hurt, pain, fear, and anger, but it existed within me. I just had to choose to exercise it.

In 2018, I had the honor of attending the red-carpet premiere of the Marvel movie *Thor: Ragnarok* and interviewing the cast, directors and producers. One of the interviews was with the New Zealand-born Taika Waititi, the director of the film. As he shared how he landed the job as director, I connected with the man, person, and enthusiast who had such a love for "colorful comics" and bringing them to life.

Some people hold the belief that no one knows what you need to be happy other than yourself. Well, I beg to differ. Taika knew that, when he is himself, it is easier to see what is truly important to you *and* others. He had the courage to allow the cast to be themselves as well. I believe it was due to the freedom he has just being himself. When I asked him if there was any performance that particularly surprised him, he answered, "My favorite is Chris's [Chris Hemsworth's] performance [as Thor] because just knowing how fun, how funny and charming he is makes you feel like, 'Oh, man if you actually were Thor, I would totally come and be with you.' I love having the opportunity to give him free range to just be himself and to be charming and to be the favorite character. In particular, when he and Mark [Ruffalo, who played the Hulk] are together, bouncing off each other, I love that."

Why is that comment from Taika so important? Sometimes I forget that I will never please myself if I am constantly trying to please other people, even if they are my son or my husband. Other times it may be my mom, the moms in my Facebook group, or the other moms at Chance's school. Giving myself permission (as Taika did with the cast) to be myself freely is my way of showing the world the beauty of what makes me unique. I have not always felt that no one can beat being me. Perhaps you've felt that way as well. People have said, "You are the only you," and in the moment, I agreed and gave my stamp of approval. But I did not always believe it. I had to work hard to be courageous and decide to be myself freely. When I heard Taika say that he "loved" giving the talent free range to be themselves, I immediately knew I wanted to focus on that quote and share the importance of giving yourself free range to be yourself.

As I began to be more honest with myself, I gained more confidence. Has that ever happened to you? I have realized life is too short not to be myself fully. When I'm being my true self:

- I am fearless, my confidence shines bright.

- I am less concerned with how others feel about me.

- I am naturally more attractive.

Taika knew that, if he allowed the already talented actors the freedom to be themselves, he would get the best of who they are on the screen. That is also true when it comes to you and me. Freedom is experienced when we are no longer held captive to the past.

Once I hatched, I had to step away from the familiarity of my past, or it would have held me back. I had to stop depending on the predictable resources I was used to. I had to embrace the new consciousness that came with the next level of growth. It all came true for me when I hatched from my familiar "egg" of fundraising, and it will be the same for you when you leave the comfort of the "egg" you are dwelling inside. The egg will become a part of your past when you hatch and realize that your future is always forward. To fully soar, continually live free from the past, and embrace the new possibilities that lie ahead of you. The sight of the eagle soaring is symbolic of your spirit.

> *"Life is a journey, not a destination."*
>
> —Ralph Waldo Emerson

For so many of us, life is about the pursuit of success, and that success has largely been defined as reaching a certain place or having a set amount of money or status.

Mother Teresa, the Catholic saint, led a life that reflected minimalism. At a very young age, she dedicated her life to God, living a life of celibacy and frugality. She was an extremely powerful and passionate person, and the individuals and families that she served always commented about her jovial spirit and authentic compassion. Many leaders, laymen and religious alike, judge their success on their conversion rate. That was not the case with Mother Teresa. In her autobiography, she said her job was not to change a Hindu or Muslim to a Catholic. Instead, it was to help a Muslim to be a better Muslim, help a Hindu to be a better Hindu, and to help a Catholic be a better Catholic. She inspired many world leaders, from the Pope to the US President, to be more compassionate, conscious, and giving, especially to individual citizens. In doing so, she found an incredible amount of real success that few philanthropists experience. She soared, and in fact still soars, pointing out to everyone who knew of her what it looks like to be successful as a human.

Another inspiring example of true success is Ms. Mary McLeod Bethune. Born the fifteenth of seventeen children to parents who were former slaves, Mary Jane McLeod grew up in rural South Carolina and attended segregated mission schools.

At eleven years old, she was given an opportunity to walk ten miles a day to attend school. She excelled there and consequently earned a scholarship to the Moody Bible Institute, where she continued to be an excellent student. She initially wanted to go to Africa to be a missionary; however, upon her graduation, the Presbyterian Board of Missions informed her that it did not send Blacks to Africa to do mission work, so she turned to education.

After marrying Albertus Bethune in 1898, she moved to Florida. In Daytona, she saw the shambles of the Black community there, and the story goes that she felt a greater calling begin to spring forth. Her desire became to establish a school and inspire the people around her to live a better quality of life. To accomplish the vision that was rising within her, she worked a full-time job and then, in the evening, sold cakes and pies to save money until she was able to open up a one-room school in 1904, called the Daytona Educational and Industrial School for Negro Girls. She was the school's one and only teacher.

In 1923, the school merged with the all-male Cookman Institute of Jacksonville, Florida, and eventually became Bethune-Cookman College, a four-year, coeducational institution. Bethune served as the college's president until 1942 and again from 1946–47.

Mary McLeod Bethune soared! She became an advisor to other educators, leaders, and even presidents. Her educational model swept through the country and impacted the lives of students from Texas to Ohio. Known as the "First Lady of the Struggle," she devoted her career to improving the lives of African Americans, first through education and political and economic empowerment, then as a top Black administrator in President Franklin D. Roosevelt's administration. Her success was not in the amount of money she left in her bank account, but rather in the amount of hope she instilled in the millions of children across the country.

Of course, this does not happen to everyone, but the lesson to learn is that hatching, leaping, and soaring is not about reaching just one goal. It is about tapping into your ideas and acting on them continually. It is about always seeking new places of discovery, growth, and ultimate freedom.

I specifically remember a time long after I launched my Motivated Mom platform and had orchestrated several tours. I was attending one of the biggest Latinx events of the year, Hispanicize, as a brand influencer for a major financial service company. I decided to join a few of the other influencers for dinner to try Cuban food for the first time. The conversation about the food sparked a discussion around nationality, and where everyone was born.

Just listening to the pride, honor, and love that the five other women at the table carried for their countries and families was incredible and something to be admired. I sat there in absolute awe, thinking, *How powerful!* They asked me, "What is your nationality? Where were you born?"

Their questions caused me great concern, not because they were difficult or unrealistic, but because I did not know the answers. I was slightly upset, and frankly embarrassed, that I had no clue about the history of my ancestors. I told them that, though I was born in the United States, I did not know my genetic composition, so I was forced to select African American when answering questionnaires about heritage because I did not know where my roots originated. I had been wondering about my heritage for years, always saying to myself, *I would love to know my nationality, who I am.*

I did not even realize the depth of my concern until I was having a conversation with my blog coach Elayna after attending Hispanicize. She was explaining how most Latinas get very offended if you misidentify their nationality. If they are Brazilian and you mistake them for Dominican, they feel slighted; not because the other nationality is less than, but because they have pride in their birthrights.

And while I'm proud to be an African American woman, I wanted to know more about my genetic make-up. A few weeks later, I found myself borderline depressed. I felt as if I was fading and not the person I had become. It took weeks to break free from that awful feeling. I could not put my finger on the problem, but I knew I had one.

Has that ever happened to you? Have you ever felt as if something was not sitting right with you and the world, but not really sure how to define it? That was me. I tried to explain my conundrum to a few people close to me, but I could not do so properly. Then it hit me. The journey to find out more about who I was from a DNA standpoint was not enough. I needed to find out more about who I was in this particular season of my life.

I was trying so hard to pursue my purpose, and somehow, I kept getting pulled back into the hustle of *just* making money. I continued working for a paycheck because my purpose was not sustainable yet. The weight of my work literally stopped me from writing my weekly blog post. I was stuck. That place of uncertainty caused me great grief. I overanalyzed and underplanned, which left me exhausted. The feeling of depression was real; I was not imagining it. I told myself, *It's okay not to be okay. But it's not okay to stay that way.*

There were three things I realized and deemed noteworthy during this experience. When you do not know who you are:

- You will begin filling that void with things and people that are not in alignment with your dreams and goals.

- You will lack confidence in your purpose, talents and abilities to fulfill your destiny.

- You will start settling for anything in hopes of having something.

This was a time of true struggle for me. Sharing this story with others was a critical part of my healing. Just seeing it on paper made me feel great. Having the knowledge that I did not have to pretend to be perfect while discovering who I was at my core was invigorating. I discovered I must always take inventory and assess how my environment affected who I was becoming.

I was living at my maximum capacity and could do no more or less than what I was doing at the time. Regardless, I still had questions.

Was I staying true to my roots? My core? Or was I feeling stuck because I was taking on the identity of my lack of purpose? I decided to order a DNA test to find out more about my heritage. When I received the results, I learned that I am a mixed bag, with ancestors flung far and wide: 34 percent Congo, 21 percent Wales, 17 percent Central America (Belize/Honduras), 10 percent Ivory Coast, 8 percent Scotland, 6 percent Europe, 1 percent North America, 1 percent Senegal, 1 percent Sardinia. That is a lot of ancestry to digest, right? And, while I cannot say exactly where I am from like the Latinas from the Hispanicize dinner, every day I am finding out more about who I am. I loved and welcomed the process that it took to get to the very core of the person that I desired to be.

With all the principles and practices that it takes to hatch, leap, and soar, it may become easy to overlook self-discipline. That is why I want to take a moment here to say that self-discipline may be one of the most important parts of reaching your pinnacle! Just as dribbling is essential to playing basketball and running is fundamental to playing tennis, self-discipline is an essential element of hatching, leaping, and soaring.

If not for self-discipline, you could become complacent and lower your head, rather than raising it to hatch. You could have retreated in fear and listened to the self-criticizing voices and negative forecasts instead of leaping into flight. You would have never discarded the excess buddies, bad habits, and emotional baggage necessary to soar, if not for self-discipline. Once you have learned your own cadence and established a habit of self-discipline in your life, grow in it and make it a part of your culture.

Soaring = True Happiness

I believe to soar in any area of your life is to have true happiness. To soar is to have gone through the hatching phase of breaking through, the leaping phase of giving it a try, and then we soar.

> *"People who soar are those who refuse to sit back and wish things would change."*
>
> —Charles R. Swindoll

To soar means that you are doing it. Whatever "it" may be, you have overcome obstacles, barriers, and challenges, and have come to a place where you are soaring.

What are the essential items that you need to carry with you?

_____

_____

_____

_____

_____

What will help you take time to focus on things that concern your inner well-being?

_____

_____

_____

_____

_____

What steps can you take to learn the words "No, I cannot do it"?

_____

_____

_____

_____

_____

Conclusion

"Change your thoughts, and you change your world."

—Norman Vincent Peale

G rowing up, I distinctly remember a few gifts that my mom bought for me that helped shape my whole life.

The first present I clearly remember from my mom was a children's Bible. I recall thinking that it was the most unexpected and special gift that I could have ever received, and I never forgot that it came from her. I was nine years old when she gave me the Bible for Christmas. I had no idea that this gift would be the cornerstone of the most important relationship in my life. I am who I am today because I believe in the words written in the very first book I remember getting from my mom. I did not realize it then, but she gave me the gift of salvation.

The second gift that meant so much to me was my FedEx sweatshirt. My brother and I received matching sweatshirts with the FedEx logo and the saying, Absolutely, Positively Overnight. This was one of the first Christmases that I had celebrated with my mom in a while. She was working at FedEx at the time. We were so proud of our shirts and proud of our mom; her hard work was paying off. We wore those shirts out; my brother even had his school pictures taken in his. It was a time of bonding and one of the best Christmases ever. I learned the value of hard work, and to never stop believing in the power of love. My mom gave me the gift of unconditional love.

The third gift was a pair of Gucci boots, which were so timely. I was transitioning from middle school to high school, and it was a tough period in my life, like it is for so many kids. I was having issues with acne, I was super skinny (which I would love to be now), and I did not feel like I fit in. Those boots were everything to me at the time. I remember wearing them to school and I felt like I was immediately *in*…but was I really? I learned a valuable lesson about friendship that year, but, more importantly, I learned to never base my value or worth, and certainly not friendships, on material things. My mom gave me the gift of self-worth.

Remember that the relationship history between my mom and me was a distant one, to say the least. So these gifts, which seemed to be her love language—or the way she showed love—had a significant impact on who I am today. They also remind me of the gifts that I intend to give or leave my son. I will be there for him, and not just for Christmas or birthdays, and I plan to give him the type of gifts that will bring out the best parts of him.

These stories have a lot to do with the entire theme of this book. As I continue to hatch, leap, and soar, I am seeking to understand moments, experiences, people, and places that have changed my life. In doing so, they have all influenced my perspective. Motherhood is not easy; it is a lot of work. And while I was not always in my mom's presence, her presents benefited me greatly, and I am grateful.

Your perspectives hold all the power when it comes to determining your tomorrows. In the words of Norman Vincent Peale, a popular minister and author, "Change your thoughts, and you change your world." It is my hope that you have not only changed your thoughts, but you've discovered the areas in your life where you need to hatch, leap, and soar in order to change your world.

Becoming the person you were created to be is not about inserting a title before or after your name, whether it is doctor, lawyer, or chief bottle washer. It is an ever-evolving process and a choice you often make over and over again. Hatching, leaping, and soaring can happen in your life, even when you do not realize it. And they can happen all at the same time.

It is all about looking inside yourself and identifying the feelings and qualities that make you who you are, like kindness, giving, ambition, loving—the list goes on and on. When all of those traits come together, they create the best version of you. I do not mean the self-centered you, who is only concerned about how many people liked your Facebook or Twitter post. No, I am talking about the you who has those irresistible urges to live more fully, to do better, to live the life that belongs to you. It is the *something* within you at your core, beyond the fear and doubt, that has not been limited by your experiences or destroyed by your mistakes and pain. It is the *something* that makes you so completely unique.

I do not need to mold my life into a façade of someone else's, and neither should you. You will continue to hatch by breaking away from things that feel easy or comfortable. There are more meaningful lessons, like believing more fully in yourself. Find the courage to leap today. Do not wait for the perfect time. Where you are now is the place to begin. Become exactly who you were created to be by constantly going through the process of self-examination and discovery.

There was a time in my life when I was going, going, going… but I did not end up anywhere that let me feel fulfilled. This churning had taken me away completely from the simplistic, easy-going, funny, relaxed person that I was in my heart. I remember feeling so stuck and bound. I was bound by non-belief, and it took me a while to decide that I wanted out of the bondage, even if that meant achieving less money and having less influence; I wanted more of me. I had to listen to the desires of my heart and follow them: not money, not popularity, not a big ego, but the music of my heart. I've heard that if you listen to peace, you will experience it. If you listen for the truth, you will hear it. If you listen for power, you will receive it. If you listen for love, you will always have it.

You will not be robbing someone when you discover and become your own good thing. No one is harmed if you are happy and living in your prosperous truth, even though sometimes finding your strength may feel like you are taking away from someone else. That is why taking the time to know yourself will enable you to better see a powerful contributor at the very essence of your being.

Being happy is a decision which seems pretty simple, but it is so much harder to actually live by. It is your responsibility to find ways to allow yourself to be happy. Your happiness can often be reflected by mood, which is directly impacted by decisions. Taking responsibility for your happiness ensures that you are happy in spite of circumstances.

I have discovered that what makes me most happy is what makes me most happy. It is just that simple. I have tried copying what others do to get to the next level. I have tried acting on what others *thought* I should do. But it comes down to acting on what *I* know I should do. When I focus on what I really love doing, that is when I am happiest. And then it is not stressful. It is like imagining that I am in my favorite place on earth every day. I am just happy.

Studies have proven that, if you believe that you are not enough, you will make it true, if only to yourself. Perception is powerful, and I have changed my perspective on many areas of my life. I now believe that I am worthy, capable, and smart, and that I definitely make a difference. And wouldn't you know, my mind is looking for ways to ensure that my life reflects what I perceive. When I began focusing on the people that could help me versus those who have hurt me, I began hatching, leaping, and soaring. I am becoming what I desire to be. And that is powerful! Everyone wants the desires of their heart. Your desires are your most powerful feeling. It is the driving force that will help you hatch, soar, and leap from the guise of a doer into a true disruptor. You will finally be able to:

- Disrupt old thoughts and behaviors that used to keep you trapped in your shell.

- Disrupt the fear that kept you from pushing toward the life you wanted and deserved.

- Disrupt the limitations that kept you heavy and weighed down, the limitations that prevented you from reaching exponential heights of happiness and fulfillment.

In truth, all of us struggle at one time or another, especially in resisting the desire to be affirmed by someone else's opinion. You may have been guilty of outwardly seeking the approval of parents, spouses, friends, and all the rest. I have certainly been in your shoes. This struggle can happen at the same time you are on the road to rejecting the constraints that come with living your life to please others. When all of the voices on the outside are vying to mold and shape your path, learn to hear, trust, and rely on the voice within you that is urging you to discover your *own* path and to become your *own* good work!

One of the subtleties that you may become aware of at the earliest stages of hatching is the joy experienced when serving others. I have found that success is deepened by this, and is otherwise empty when it is only self-seeking. Fame is often fleeting when it does not help to connect others to opportunities that otherwise could not happen. Success without serving is hard to fathom for me, as is success without relationships. What I have come to know about those who successfully soar is that they connect, uplift, share, and empower others with enthusiasm along the way.

I was guilty of taking on clients and jobs for the money. The sole focus on monetary gain eventually completely overwhelmed me, and I ended up sick, stressed, and so unhappy that I began taking it out on my family. When I started cutting clients and saying no to things that did not align with my mental schema, I became freer to focus on and enjoy the things that were set before me to do. This is now the lens through which I filter everything in my life. I feel better and happier about everything in my life these days.

I had to skinny down and prioritize who I wanted to be, what I wanted to do, and how those decisions made me feel. When

I changed my focus and stopped thinking about money, position, or power, I found the opportunities I was looking for. They were the ones that made me most happy and aligned with who I was at my core. They were right in front of me. And it is the same for you; you may be blind to them right now, because you have not tapped into your true potential that is hidden at your core.

It is difficult work to become who you were created to be. At least it was for me. I am doing great things, but at times, I still feel unhappy. A small part of that is due to a real disease that I am working through called depression. But part of the process is to keep asking myself, *Why am I depressed?* Remember, I am still hatching, leaping, and soaring in many areas of my life. I hope to never stop.

Hatching, leaping, and soaring is a process. It is a constant assessment of self, which is a huge challenge. Let's face it, most of us clearly remember our worst mistakes, most public blunders, and secret silent fears. Put another way, we know our imperfections quite well. Instead of dwelling on the past, you should try to remember that no human is perfect and not one of us will be called out for imperfection. Because, while perfection is unattainable, excellence is very doable. Plainly put, excellence is consistently doing the very best you can do at all times.

As I look back, I am so thankful for all that I have learned during my first round of hatching, leaping, and soaring. I say the first round because now I know that this trilogy is not something that happens just one time; it is a way of life! In order to be a person who is truly fulfilled, happy, and able to enjoy the fruitfulness of success, you have to remain the kind of person who is constantly open to growing and living with passion. Since I broke out of my own comfort zone of complacency, I am content living as a passionate person. I always want to know that I am making a difference. Having a sense of fulfillment is very important to me.

Then there is the desire to live the life that you believe you were created for. Passion makes complacency uncomfortable. When you live your gift and do what you love, you will thrive. Once you allow the gifts that live inside of you to break out, you will begin to close the door on that which does not align with your core passions. You will arrive in a place that is not determined by a dollar figure, but by the difference you make in the lives of others. Do what you are purposed and passionate about. This is the ultimate time when your *work* is combined with your *advocacy.*

You are right if you think that this changeover does not happen overnight. I have made a lot of progress, but I still have a lot to learn. But with hard work, dedication, faith, and the belief that you can…your transformation does not have to take long. Your gifts will take you through and bring you into a place of total fulfillment, true happiness, and real success!

Anyone can *hatch, leap,* and *soar* to become who they were created to be and to fulfill their own purpose. Anyone can be successful in life, despite their upbringing or their past. Open up to all the new possibilities that you can achieve, and take that leap of faith that will enable you to soar to new heights. Anything is possible for you.

Acknowledgments

There are so many people to thank, people who have contributed to my life and made it so much better. First, I would like to thank my amazing husband, Andre, and son, Chance, for supporting me as I hatched to become a better version of myself, leaped to pursue the desires of my heart, and soared into the fullness of true happiness.

I'd like to thank my parents for giving me life. I'm especially thankful for my mom; she is one of the strongest women I know, and I am honored to be her daughter. To my very first reason to be a good example, my little brother Donte. He made me responsible, patient, loving, and a fighter—as I had to finish fights he started all the time!!! To ALL of my other siblings (too many to name), I love you all to life and am so thankful to have you in my life.

Thanks also to Deborah Hauss and Candace Fleming for their helpful feedback and editing skills. Last but certainly not least, to the phenomenal Motivated Moms, especially LaSonia Lurry, Michelle Williams, Loretta Dozier, Jewel Cade, Jo Copper, and Andreyetta Dennis who inspired me to be the person I am today. Thank you for caring…it mattered a whole lot!

About the Author

LaToyia Dennis is a mom, wife, speaker, author, early childhood education advocate, parent enthusiast, and master motivator. With more than fifteen years of experience in development, strategic planning, and nonprofit management, she is the founder and principal fundraising consultant of the nonprofit organization A Chance to Learn, as well as the founder and driving force behind the program/platform, The Motivated Mom.

Founded in 2011, A Chance to Learn is dedicated to finding and providing solutions to enhance families through the empowerment of women and quality education for children. For more information, visit www.achancetolearn.org.

The Motivated Mom, Inc., is a nonprofit organization dedicated to helping moms live a life of purpose with abundance and financial freedom. The platform encompasses an uplifting and informative blog, programs to help moms become self-sufficient and become Mompreneurs, and a host of events, including our signature Motivated Mom Retreat. For more information, visit www.motivatedmom.org.

LaToyia served as the principal consultant, relationship manager, and nonprofit manager at LaToyia Dennis &

Company, a full-service fundraising consulting, program development, and management boutique firm. After several years of service, LaToya decided to combine her expertise with her passion for moms and launched PhilMOMthropy, which celebrates motherhood and social good. PhilMOMthropy provides support to moms as they give back to their local communities through nonprofit organizations, community engagement, meaningful partnerships, and lasting impact. Please visit www.philmomthropy.org.

LaToyia was the first in her family to obtain an advanced degree when she graduated with an MBA in nonprofit management from the University of Dallas. Above all, LaToyia is a dedicated mother to her son, Chance, and a loyal wife to her husband of twelve years, Andre.